ARCHIVAL AND SECONDARY DATA

THE SAGE QUANTITATIVE RESEARCH KIT

Archival and Secondary Data Analysis by *Tarani Chandola* and *Cara Booker* is the 5th volume in *The SAGE Quantitative Research Kit*. This book can be used together with the other titles in the *Kit* as a comprehensive guide to the process of doing quantitative research, but is equally valuable on its own as a practical introduction to Data Archives and Secondary Data Analysis.

Editors of The SAGE Quantitative Research Kit:

Malcolm Williams – *Cardiff University, UK*

Richard D. Wiggins – *UCL Social Research Institute, UK*

D. Betsy McCoach – *University of Connecticut, USA*

Founding editor:

The late W. Paul Vogt – *Illinois State University, USA*

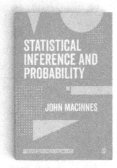

ARCHIVAL AND SECONDARY DATA

TARANI CHANDOLA
CARA BOOKER

Los Angeles | London | New Delhi
Singapore | Washington DC | Melbourne

THE SAGE QUANTITATIVE RESEARCH KIT

Los Angeles | London | New Delhi
Singapore | Washington DC | Melbourne

SAGE Publications Ltd
1 Oliver's Yard
55 City Road
London EC1Y 1SP

SAGE Publications Inc.
2455 Teller Road
Thousand Oaks, California 91320

SAGE Publications India Pvt Ltd
B 1/I 1 Mohan Cooperative Industrial Area
Mathura Road
New Delhi 110 044

SAGE Publications Asia-Pacific Pte Ltd
3 Church Street
#10-04 Samsung Hub
Singapore 049483

Editor: Jai Seaman
Assistant editor: Charlotte Bush
Production editor: Manmeet Kaur Tura
Copyeditor: QuADS Prepress Pvt Ltd
Proofreader: Derek Markham
Indexer: Cathryn Pritchard
Marketing manager: Susheel Gokarakonda
Cover design: Shaun Mercier
Typeset by: C&M Digitals (P) Ltd, Chennai, India

Library of Congress Control Number: 2021935561

British Library Cataloguing in Publication data

A catalogue record for this book is available from the British Library

ISBN 978-1-5264-2472-3

CONTENTS

List of Figures and Tables ix

About the Authors xiii

1 What Is Archival and Secondary Data Analysis? **1**

Background and History 2

Secondary Data Analysis: What Does It Mean? 3

Why Should I Do Research on Second-Hand Data? 3

The Ontological and Epistemological Issues of Secondary Analysis 4

The Social Construction of Data 5

Useful Concepts and Terms in Secondary Analysis 6

 Data and Theory 6

 Secondary Data Analysis Versus Big Data Analysis 6

 Metadata, Paradata and Secondary Data 7

 Data and Variables 8

2 From Ideas to Research Questions **11**

Background 12

Research Questions to Research Design 12

Coming Up With a Research Topic 13

Concepts and Variables 14

Choices and Compromise 15

How Do Your Concepts Relate 16

Population and Units of Analysis 17

3 Finding Secondary Data **21**

Background 22

Your Ideal Data Set 22

Looking for Research Data 25

 Starting Your Search for Research Data 25

 Search Tool 1: Searching for a Particular Data Set Within the UKDS 26

 Search Tool 2: Key Data Within the UKDS 27

 Search Tool 3: Theme Pages Within the UKDS 27

 Search Tool 4: The UKDS Data Catalogue 27

 What Happens If You Get Too Many Results? 27

 Who Can Access the Data? 28

Keywords, Search Terms and Databases   28
Practical Steps in Searching for Data   29

4   Getting to Know the Data   **33**

Background   34
Interpreting Data Correctly   34
   Evaluating the Data Catalogue Entry   34
   Establishing the Coverage, Universe and Methodology of the Data   36
   Exploring the Survey Documentation   40
Using Nesstar to explore data   42

5   Basic Data Management   **47**

Background   48
Basic Data Manipulation Commands in the Statistical Software
Packages SPSS and STATA   48
   Using a Syntax or Command File   48
   Basic SPSS Commands   49
   Basic STATA Commands   49
Building a Usable Data Set   50
   Creating Subsets of Data   50
   Wide or Long Data Sets?   50
Common Problems With Getting Familiar With Secondary Data Sets   52
Tips on Handling Secondary Data Sets   53
Getting to Know the Understanding Society Data Set   57
   Why Use the Understanding Society Data Set?   57
   Contents of the Study   58
   Target Population and Samples   58
   Accessing the Data   59
   Using the Data   59
   Data Structure   59
Practical Exercise   63
   Understanding Society Common STATA Commands   63
   Commonly Used Commands to Explore Data   64
   Commonly Used Commands to Modify and Sort the Data File   65
   Commonly Used Commands to Summarise Data   65

6   Manipulating Data and Basic Statistical Analysis   **69**

Background   70
Examining Univariate Distributions   70
   Example   71
Examining Bivariate Associations   77

Manipulating Data		77
Cross Tabulations		79
Comparing Means		83
Statistical Tests to Compare Means and Proportions		84
Examining Multivariate Associations		87
Making Statistical Inference		87
What Is Weighting? How Do You Use the Derived Weights?		88
Basic Longitudinal Data Analysis		93
Examples of Longitudinal Data		93
Examining Associations Between Variables Measured at Different Times		93
Describing Change in a Repeated Measure		94
Modelling Change in a Repeated Measure		94
Practical Longitudinal Data Analysis Exercise		95
Data Management		95
Descriptive Analysis		100
Regression Analysis		102

7	**Writing Up Your Analyses**	**107**
	Background	108
	Existing Guidelines	108
	Reporting Your Results in Words	110
	Preparing Tables	111
	Preparing Graphs	111
	Practical Exercise	112

8	**Complexities of Working With Secondary Data: Limitations of Archival and Secondary Data Analysis**	**119**
	Background	120
	Identifying Problems and Limitations in Secondary Data	120
	Using Derived Variables	122
	Dealing With Missing Data	123
	Changing Your Research Questions	126
	Showing Critical Awareness	127
	Sharing Your Analyses and Coding	128

9	**Conclusions**	**131**
	Next Steps in Secondary Data Analysis	132
	Critics of Secondary Analysis	133
	Ethical Risks and Informed Consent, Confidentiality and Anonymity	133
	The Future of Secondary Data	134

Appendix 1:   *Case Study Example of Secondary Data Analysis Using Biomarker Data From Understanding Society, the UK Household Longitudinal Study*   137

Appendix 2:   *Software and Data Used in This Book and Related User Guides*   157

Glossary   159

References   163

Index   165

LIST OF FIGURES AND TABLES

List of figures

2.1   Independent and dependent variables   18

4.1   Screenshot from the UK Data Service Nesstar resource on the distribution of 'How satisfied are you with: Your present job?' from the data Set European Quality of Life Time Series, 2011   43

4.2   Screenshot from the UK Data Service Nesstar resource on the cross tabulation of 'How satisfied are you with: Your present job?' by 'Is your household able to make ends meet?' from the data Set European Quality of Life Time Series, 2011   44

6.1   Distribution of b_depenth 'feels tense about job' from wave 2 of Understanding Society   72

6.2   Distribution of b_dvage 'age' from wave 2 of Understanding Society   74

6.3   Histogram of combined job stress measure by categories of highest education qualification   85

7.1   Histogram of household income   113

7.2   Scatter plot of Age and HH_income   115

7.3   Scatter plot of household income and age   116

A1.1   Histogram of educational qualifications   143

A1.2   Histogram of social class   144

List of tables

5.1   Example of a 'wide' data set with one record/person per row   51

5.2   Example of a 'long' data set with multiple rows of data for each person   51

5.3   Key data files for analysing data for responding households and individuals in Understanding Society and the British Household Panel Study   60

5.4   Missing value codes in Understanding Society and the
      British Household Panel Study   61
5.5   Key variables in the Understanding Society data sets   62

6.1   Distribution of b_sex 'sex' at wave 2 of Understanding Society   75
6.2   Distribution of b_depenth1 'feels tense about job' at wave 2 of
      Understanding Society   75
6.3   Distribution of b_hiqual_dv 'highest qualification' at wave 2 of
      Understanding Society   76
6.4   Distribution of b_dvage 'age' at wave 2 of Understanding Society   76
6.5   Cross tabulation of sex and b_depenth1 'feels tense about job'
      at wave 2 of Understanding Society: row percentages   80
6.6   Cross tabulation of sex and b_depenth1 'feels tense about
      job' at wave 2 of Understanding Society: column percentages   80
6.7   Correlation of the job stress variables from wave 2
      of Understanding Society   82
6.8   Mean of the combined job stress measure by highest
      education qualification from wave 2 of Understanding Society   84
6.9   Analysis of variance of the combined job stress measure by
      highest education qualification from wave 2 of Understanding Society 84
6.10 Multiple comparison (Scheffé) analysis of variance of the
      combined job stress measure by highest education qualification
      from wave 2 of Understanding Society   86
6.11 Weighted analysis of variance of the combined job stress measure
      by highest education qualification from wave 2 of
      Understanding Society   91
6.12 Survey weighted mean of the combined job stress measure by
      highest education qualification from wave 2 of Understanding Society 92
6.13 Descriptive statistics of socio-demographic characteristics
      at Understanding Society wave 1   101
6.14 Parameter estimates from the regression model of GHQ-12   103

7.1   Subsample ($n = 25$) of four variables taken from one of the waves
      of Understanding Society   112
7.2   STATA output from tabstat command   114
7.3   Mean and standard deviation (SD) of household income by
      highest qualifications and sex   114

A1.1 Frequencies of IgM and IgG   144
A1.2 Means of continuous biomarkers   145

A1.3   Frequencies of IgM by educational qualifications   146

A1.4   Frequencies of IgG by educational qualifications   146

A1.5   Frequencies of IgM by social class   147

A1.6   Frequencies of IgG by social class   148

A1.7   Means of biomarkers by educational qualification   149

A1.8   Means of biomarkers by social class   149

A1.9   Descriptive statistics of biomarkers by gender   150

A1.10 Linear regression estimates of selected biomarkers on
       highest educational qualifications   152

A1.11 Logistic regression odds ratios of IgM and IgG on highest
       educational qualifications   153

A1.12 Linear regression estimates of selected biomarkers on social class 154

A1.13 Logistic regression odds ratios of IgM and IgG and social class   154

ABOUT THE AUTHORS

Tarani Chandola is a Professor of medical sociology. He is the Co-director of the ESRC (Economic and Research Council) International Centre for Lifecourse Studies in Society and Health and is also the co-director for the SOC-B (Social-Biological) Centre for Doctoral Training funded by the ESRC and BBSRC (Biotechnology and Biological Sciences Research Council). He is a member of the ESRC Strategic Advisory Network, fellow of the Academy of Social Sciences and the Royal Statistical Society and is an editor-in-chief of the journal *Sociology*. His research is primarily on the social determinants of health, focusing on health inequalities and psychosocial factors and the analysis of longitudinal cohort studies.

Cara Booker is a research fellow at the Institute for Social and Economic Research at the University of Essex. She received her Ph.D. in health behaviour research from the University of Southern California. Her primary research focus is on social determinants of adolescent health and well-being. She has published several book chapters and peer-reviewed papers. Her other research interests include social determinants of health and well-being among minority populations, such as the LGBT (lesbian, gay, bisexual, and transgender) population. She has cross-sectional and longitudinal analytical expertise of social surveys and experience of interdisciplinary research.

1

WHAT IS ARCHIVAL AND SECONDARY DATA ANALYSIS?

TARANI CHANDOLA AND CARA BOOKER

Chapter Overview

Background and history 2

Secondary data analysis: what does it mean? 3

Why should I do research on second-hand data? 3

The ontological and epistemological issues of secondary analysis 4

The social construction of data 5

Useful concepts and terms in secondary analysis 6

Further Reading 8

Background and history

The image of a researcher dusting books off a shelf of a library is one that applies to many disciplines still today, but in the social sciences, much of the data today is digital and held in online digital archives. These digital data archives contain a wide range of data on different aspects of social life from many countries. These **primary data** have been collected by other researchers for their own research purposes and deposited at a data archive for other researchers to use in **secondary data** analysis. This book is a step-by-step illustration for people new to secondary data analysis to use the data sets stored in such digital data archives.

While in some disciplines there may have been some reluctance to share data by those who collect data, there is now a growing acceptance among people who collect data of the scientific value for data sharing. This acceptance has grown partly due to the remarkable advances in electronic infrastructure for archiving and sharing of such data. There has also been a drive by research funders towards promoting and facilitating the reuse and secondary analysis of data. Furthermore, primary data collectors now see considerable value in having other researchers not related to their study use the data in other contexts, for other types of research questions and also to validate and test their original analyses in the spirit of open scientific enquiry.

The UK social sciences have a long tradition of secondary data analysis which has been championed by the Economic and Social Research Council (ESRC) with funding for digital data archives such as the UK Data Service (UKDS; www.ukdataservice.ac.uk) and its previous incarnations – the UK Data Archive and the SSRC (Social Sciences Research Council) Survey Archive. In other countries, there are data archives which hold large social science data sets like the GESIS – Leibniz-Institute for the Social Sciences, which is the largest infrastructure institution for the social sciences in Germany. To find out more about other European digital data archives, you can visit the CESSDA (Consortium of European Social Science Data Archives) Consortium (www.cessda.eu/Consortium). This is a consortium of social science data archives from several European countries. In the USA, the Roper Center for Public Opinion Research (https://ropercenter.cornell.edu) holds vast amounts of public opinion data, while the Inter-University Consortium for Political and Social Research (ICPSR; www.icpsr.umich.edu/icpsrweb) is another rich source of secondary data.

In addition to these digital data archives, there are a number of high-quality cross-national social science data sets which are also available for secondary data analysis, such as the European Social Survey (www.europeansocialsurvey.org) and the Survey of Health and Retirement in Europe (www.share-project.org). Researchers based in academic institutions can often freely access these data archives and data sets through open and internet-based application procedures.

Secondary data analysis: what does it mean?

A definition of secondary analysis that is widely used is 'any further analysis of an existing data set which presents interpretations, conclusions or knowledge additional to, or different from, those presented in the first report on the inquiry as a whole and its main results' (Hakim, 1982, p. 2). Secondary analysis thus implies some sort of reanalysis of data that have already been collected and analysed.

The term *secondary analysis* is most often used in relation to survey data sets, although many other types of data are available for secondary analysis, including administrative data (which are not typically collected for research purposes) and qualitative data. Data sets that describe regions and countries such as census data sets are also available for secondary analysis. However, much of secondary data analysis is of surveys of individuals, so the secondary analysis of survey data is the main focus of this book.

A primary data source is an original document that contains first-hand information about a topic or an event. There are many different types of primary data sources, but in the social sciences, we tend to rely on data from a wide range of sources, including questionnaire and interview transcripts, video footage and photographs, historical records, blogs and social media entries, eyewitness accounts and newspaper articles.

Analysis of a secondary data source is an interpretation, discussion or evaluation of an event or issue that is based on primary source evidence. Existing survey data can be a primary data source, but they could also include reviews of other research, journal articles, abstracts and bibliographies. The differences between a primary and a secondary source can be ambiguous. A source may be primary in one context and secondary in another. Some key elements of difference are around whether the data creator/collector was part of the data analysis. If that is the case, then that is likely to be a primary data analysis.

Why should I do research on second-hand data?

You may feel that all the interesting research questions have already been answered by the researchers who collected the primary data. And it is certainly important to read their papers and reports using the data to see if they have already addressed some, if not all, of the aspects of your particular research question. But even if that were the case, there would still be some utility in doing secondary analysis because it is important to reproduce results from previous studies. It may be that you could be using different methods to address the same research question, and you may need to find out if your results differ from the primary data collector's results. Many statistical methods come with a variety of assumptions, and it is useful to analyse the same research question on the same data using a different statistical method that may not have the same set of assumptions to see if the results or inferences are robust to the assumptions underlying the statistical method.

Another big advantage in doing secondary data analysis is saving the cost of and time taken to do primary data collection. Conducting a high-quality survey on a large number of people could involve quite a lot of money, even if you use internet surveys to lower the cost of data collection. Then, there is the time spent in waiting for survey respondents to fill in their answers to questions, and then the time to get all the survey data into a manageable data file ready for analysis. Reusing data from a data archive, on the other hand, is often free for academic researchers, and most data can be downloaded instantly from data archives after filling in some details about your proposed secondary research. Much of the secondary data in digital data archives contain larger sample sizes of high-quality data than what most researchers could realistically produce themselves, saving time and resources.

While the data may be 'second hand', with a previous owner, this should not put researchers off. In fact, unlike second-hand cars, the more frequently the data are used, the greater the likelihood of the data being of high quality. Most secondary researchers will tend to stay away from data that has been badly collected or with little relevance beyond a specific research project.

The ontological and epistemological issues of secondary analysis

Secondary data analysis tends to follow a scientific paradigm which consists of the following components: ontology, epistemology and methodology. The scientific paradigm or positivism originated from studies of the natural world and has then been applied to understanding the social world (Scotland, 2012). The ontological position of data analysis is one of realism, one of the central tenets of which is that the objects of research (e.g. survey participants) have an existence independent of the researcher (e.g. the survey interviewer or a secondary data researcher). A positivist epistemology is often associated with this realist ontology. Most positivists assume that reality is not completely dependent on the subjective perceptions of the data collector, and thus, data collected by somebody else can reveal an objective reality that is independent of the person collecting the data. The positivist epistemology is one of objectivism. Data collectors can go about discovering an objective reality that is impartial to the senses and perceptions of the data collector. The researcher, data collector and the researched are independent entities. The data that is collected can be objective, valid and factual and does not solely reside in the perceptions of the data collector.

Positivists view their methodology as value neutral and deduce true relationships from the objective data. Methods such as correlation and experiments are used to reduce complex interactions between data in the discovery of new patterns or truths. Methods such as inferential statistics from secondary data sets allow the analysis of data from specific samples to be generalised to wider **populations**. Positivist research is valid if the results from researchers can be generalised/transferred to other populations or situations (**external validity**) and different researchers can arrive at the same conclusions (**replicable** and reliable).

The positivist paradigm of secondary data analysis comes with some limitations. Methods developed to understand the natural world may not always be directly transferable to the social world. Positivism attempts to reduce the complexity of the social world to a few variables and cannot completely capture all the different aspects and contexts of social life. Some key data or variables may not be known to the data collector at the time of data collection. For example, in some studies of health conducted in the first half of the 20th century, data on smoking was not collected because the relationship between smoking and ill health was not known at that time. This meant that secondary data analysis looking at health outcomes from those particular data sets were limited, because many people were smokers at that time, and this information was not collected in the data.

Positivists can also self-delude themselves into thinking that their research is 'objective' and 'value free'. However, researchers often make value-laden judgements – for example, through the selection of variables to be analysed, the data to be observed and collected and the interpretation of findings. Someone conducting research using secondary data analysis is not necessarily a positivist as they may be well aware of the limitations of the data and try to take account of these limitations when analysing the data or making inferences from the data.

The social construction of data

Any analysis of secondary data needs to explore who defined the original research topics, what methods and definitions were used in that research and what the assumptions were behind those research questions. As all data are subjective to some degree, it is important that these assumptions underpinning the original primary research are made clear and explicit to secondary researchers.

For example, while some people may view official data such as a population census as 'objective', the type of data that are collected in such official data is a result of some value-laden judgements of a committee or researchers about what are the important questions that need to be asked in that population. Furthermore, the categories of data that are collected are subject to some degree of subjectivity. For some data like ethnicity, the degree to which data on potentially small ethnic groups are collected needs to be balanced against the cost of asking such detail in the population. If you have a questionnaire with close to 100 categories of ethnicity to choose from, then that makes it difficult for people to choose the group they identify with. So there is another level of subjectivity that results in specific data being collected even in official statistics.

Another source of subjectivity is the process of data collection. Although a lot of data collection exercises use standardised methods such as an interview schedule or questionnaire and standardised methods of interacting with participants in a study, there is still room for some element of subjectivity. For example, we know that there are effects of the interviewer's race and gender on interviewees and how they respond to a survey. Moreover, the interviewer may (consciously or unconsciously) **bias** a participant's response to a set of questions. An additional source of subjectivity can come from the data analysts themselves, who select particular sets of analyses to conduct and present a selection of their research for publication or review.

The subjectivity in any survey data collection and analyses does not mean all survey data analyses are biased to the point that there is little value in doing such research. Rather, it is to point out that all research is subjective to some degree and that an awareness of this subjectivity is a necessary first step in making the assumptions underlying the data and analysis explicit.

Useful concepts and terms in secondary analysis

Data and theory

Social data and theory are intertwined. Data are empirical observations, and theories are the ideas and concepts that organise existing data. Theories are also used to make predictions about new data and what we should expect to find (or hypothesise) with new primary or secondary data that have not yet been analysed for a specific research question. Good theories and hypotheses must be strongly supported by the data. Secondary data is often very useful in testing middle-range theories and hypotheses under specific conditions. For example, a theory about how social mobility occurs may have been generated by observations (or data) from a specific country (or context). Secondary data on social mobility and the related factors from a different country could test whether the theory holds in other contexts.

Secondary data analysis versus big data analysis

Some of the secondary data sets held in data archives contain very large amounts of data, although they differ from what many people call 'big data'. Big data, like secondary data in data archives, are digital data, requiring computational resources for processes. However, most big data tend to be generated by automated processes such as administrative forms or a collection of internet-based searches and have not been processed by researchers and deposited in a data archive. Instead, big data typically requires a great deal of processing, data manipulation and editing before being analysed for research purposes. In contrast, secondary data sets from data archives have typically gone through substantial data quality checks, with available metadata (data about the data) on the survey or study design, questionnaire and variables. However, it is also becoming increasingly common for some big data to be deposited in data archives for purposes of secondary data analysis. For example, the UKDS now provides big data resources and training for researchers (www.ukdataservice.ac.uk/about-us/our-rd/big-data-network-support.aspx).

The context of data collection is an important key feature of secondary data in data archives. For example, data on the characteristics of the study population, the sampling frame, the response rate and the data collection process are usually documented in data archives. In contrast, such contextual descriptions are often missing from big data, even though a lot of social science research is about the context of the data collection.

Metadata, paradata and secondary data

Metadata and paradata are important aspects of all secondary data sets. As you have not personally collected all the data yourself, as a researcher, you are reliant on the documentation provided by the primary data collectors so that you have a good idea about the conditions and context of the primary data collection.

Metadata means 'data about data'. All the data sets available within a digital data archive will have metadata describing the contents of data sets. This metadata is usually a subset of core data documentation providing standardised structured information explaining the purpose, origin, time references, geographic location, creator, access conditions and terms of use of the survey data.

The **paradata** of a survey is data about the process by which the survey data was collected. Sometimes paradata is called 'administrative data' about the survey, with data on the times of day interviews were conducted, how long the interviews took, how many times there were contacts with each interviewee or attempts to contact the interviewee, the reluctance of the interviewee and the mode of communication (e.g. phone, Web, email or in person).

While metadata documentation is typically about the whole survey, paradata tends to be about each observation (or person) in a survey. They are very useful for survey researchers to make inferences about the costs and management of a survey, but paradata are also very useful to other researchers who use such data to make inferences about non-respondents in a survey.

Data and variables

In survey data sets, variables are the component parts of data sets representing the survey questions. In a rectangular data file, the variables are represented in columns, while each individual survey respondent is represented in a row. Usually in a survey, there can be a lot of variables which makes it difficult for someone to understand what data has been collected just by looking at the variables in the data. The description of the variables, their names and labels and the survey questions that generated the variables are usually described in the metadata.

Chapter Summary

- Secondary analysis implies some sort of re-analysis of data that have already been collected and analysed, whereas a primary data source is an original document that contains first-hand information about a topic or an event.
- Advantages of secondary analysis include the ability to reproduce results from previous studies and it is significantly cheaper and less time-consuming than primary data collection.
- Any analysis of secondary data needs to explore who defined the original research topics, what methods and definitions were used in that research and what the assumptions were behind those research questions.
- Big data is digital data requiring computational resources and tends to be generated by automated processes. In contrast, secondary data sets from data archives have typically gone through substantial data quality checks, with available metadata (data about the data) on the survey or study design, questionnaire and variables.
- Metadata and paradata are integral aspects of all secondary data sets. Metadata means 'data about data' and encompasses variables. Paradata is 'administrative data', or rather data about the process by which the survey data was collected.

Further Reading

Goodwin, J. (2012a). *Sage secondary data analysis: Vol. 1. Using secondary sources and secondary analysis*. Sage.

Hakim, C. (1982). *Secondary analysis in social research: A guide to data sources and methods with examples*. Allen & Unwin/Unwin Hyman.

Scotland, J. (2012). Exploring the philosophical underpinnings of research: Relating ontology and epistemology to the methodology and methods of the scientific, interpretive, and critical research paradigms. *English Language Teaching, 5*(9), 9–16. https://doi.org/10.5539/elt.v5n9p9

Smith, E. (2008). *Using secondary data in educational and social research* (1st ed.). Open University Press.

Stewart, D., & Kamins, M. (1993). *Secondary research*. Sage.

2

FROM IDEAS TO RESEARCH QUESTIONS

TARANI CHANDOLA

Chapter Overview

Background 12

Research questions to research design 12

Coming up with a research topic 13

Concepts and variables 14

Choices and compromise 15

How do your concepts relate 16

Population and units of analysis 17

Further Reading 19

Background

Before investigating what types of data are available for secondary analysis in digital data archives, you must first of all think about your research topic and questions. This chapter is a brief overview of the steps you need to take to arrive at a set of working research questions, which will then help you in your search for relevant secondary data. Specifying your research questions and study design is just as important for primary data researchers as it is for secondary analysis, but there are some additional complexities for researchers using secondary data which are highlighted in this chapter.

Research questions to research design

Developing your research questions is often an iterative process. In secondary data analysis, it is quite common to start your research with a particular set of research questions and end up answering a completely different set of research questions. This is quite different from data analysis using primary data you have collected for a specific purpose. In primary data analysis, the research questions are usually pre-specified. You can pre-specify the research questions for secondary data analysis as well, but given that most researchers using secondary data are unfamiliar with the data, they will often find themselves in the situation of having to revise their original research questions because the specific data or variables are not available, or there are considerable missing data or there is an unexpected feature of the secondary data that the researcher was not aware of until they started analysing the data.

For example, certain questions may only be asked of specific people, that is, mothers, elderly, people in paid work, and so on, or they may only be asked in specific schedules, that is, every other wave or every 3 years of data collection. This may result in limiting the scope or revising the original research questions and subsequent analyses.

However, the difficulties of pre-specifying a research question for secondary data analysis should not discourage researchers from having a working research question. This is usually derived from the general research area and topics of interest. Research questions are usually generated from unresolved debates and questions in the topic of interest. For example, many research papers will often conclude 'more research is needed on . . . ', ? specifying further topics of research as well as justifying why further research is needed. This implies that the researcher first has to do a lot of reading around their research topic. This is vital as the relevant research literature gives researchers important insights into their topic, ? such as what is already known and what the commonly used research methods and data are. Research questions may be very broad to begin with, but they can be refined and developed as you progress.

When you have a clear idea of your research questions, selecting a suitable research design will become easier. However, you may find initial research questions need further thought, clarification and elaboration as you become more familiar with what is already known on the topic and what remains to be answered.

Coming up with a research topic

Finding your own research topic is something that is often driven by your own interests. You may have your own questions about why things are as they are, or how things can change. Using your own curiosity about the social world is perhaps the strongest way of defining both your research topic and questions.

My own research area is mainly about stress and health. While there has been a lot of work on the topic for many years now, there are still new things to discover. As someone who may be new to the field, it is always good to do some initial reading about a topic to see if there is anything in it that interests you. Most people start with an internet search on the topic ('stress and health'). One of the top findings from a Google search on 'stress and health' is something from the American Psychological Association website (www.apa.org/helpcenter/stress.aspx):

> Chronic stress: When stress starts interfering with your ability to live a normal life for an extended period, it becomes even more dangerous. The longer the stress lasts, the worse it is for both your mind and body. You might feel fatigued, unable to concentrate or irritable for no good reason, for example. But chronic stress causes wear and tear on your body, too.

Given the existing research evidence summarised above, you may be interested in potentially unanswered questions such as those related to causality (Does stress really cause poorer health or is it something else that is causing poor health? Will reducing stress lead to better health?), mechanisms (How does stress cause poorer health?) or interventions (How can you reduce stress?). All of these potential research questions need further reading on existing research to see if there are debates/issues that remain unanswered. There are many online resources on how to do a literature review. The literature will help to show you how other researchers have understood and defined key terms and concepts for your research topic.

Once you have decided on a research topic and related question, you will need to see what data you need in order to answer the research question. In some academic disciplines, it may be entirely possible to answer a research question without resorting to data. You may also discover that it is entirely feasible to answer your question collecting your own primary data. However, as is often the case with empirical research questions, we wish to generalise our findings to wider population, which is why secondary data analysis of large population-based surveys are crucial to answering some types of research questions.

Concepts and variables

When doing social research, you need to define your key terms and concepts. Having a clear idea of key terms and concepts is very important for working out how they can be measured in your research. The literature review you do will give you insights into the strengths and weaknesses of common ways of measuring key concepts. For the secondary analysis of existing quantitative data, you also need to think critically about what those variables actually measure.

For example, what do we mean by 'stress and health'? Both 'stress' and 'health' mean different things to different people and can be measured in different ways. For example, people often say they are feeling stressed, which could be a valid response to a survey question on 'how stressed are you feeling'. However, people also talk about specific domains of stress like work stress or the stress of debt. Here, it is useful to distinguish between the 'stressors', or the condition that generates the work stress (like insecure working conditions) or financial stress (like not having enough money to pay your bills), and the 'stress response', which is often an emotional response to the stressor. Also, the stress response could be a biological response – the activation of the body's 'fight or flight' response to cope with a stressful situation. This means a stress response could also be measured in terms of biological data (see Appendix 1 for some examples), as well as through responses to a survey question.

Similarly, health is a multidimensional concept that can be measured in different ways. For example, questions related to mental health are not the same as those related to physical health. For some people, a question on 'disability' could measure health, whereas for other researchers, disability is not a direct measure of health. For instance, many people with some limited functional abilities report having excellent health. When thinking about relating the concepts of 'stress and health', it is also important to keep in mind related concepts such as 'depression'. For some people, being depressed and stressed mean the same thing, but actually in the research literature, they are quite different. Someone who is under stress may not be depressed. That is why it is really important to have accurate and valid questions related to your specific research topic, so that people respond appropriately (e.g. reporting their stress levels rather than reporting how depressed they are).

In a typical data set, you will find a number of 'variables', most of which are derived from survey questions. Sometimes those variables are direct representations of a survey question. For example, the survey question, 'How stressed are you feeling?'

could be represented by a variable called *stress* with numbers related to the response categories of the survey question ('Extremely', 'Very', 'A little', 'Not at all'). As a researcher, you need to assess to what extent this survey question is a good measure of your research topic of interest.

You may think this question about stress is a valid measure of stress. However, you may also be worried that it is very subjective. How do you know that one person's rating of their stress correspond to someone else's rating of their stress? You may also be worried about the response categories. To what extent will these categories mean the same thing to different people? You may also be concerned that someone's response to that particular stress question may be affected by their mood, so their response is not really a measure of their stress but really a measure of how unhappy or depressed they are feeling.

Choices and compromise

As a researcher, you will often need to make some difficult choices in terms of the secondary data sets you select. Some of the data sets will have detailed questions and data on one aspect of your research topic, but they may not include such detailed data on other aspects of your topic. If this was primary research, it wouldn't be such a problem as you can decide for yourself what the most important questions are to include in your survey. As a secondary data researcher, you are limited to the questions that someone else thought were important.

Many key social science concepts are complex and difficult to measure. Researchers invest lots of time and resources in developing appropriate measures. As a result, you will often find similar and standardised approaches to measuring certain concepts and when such data and questions are available. For example, there are a number of well-established and validated survey questionnaires related to health, such as the SF-36 (Short Form Survey with 36 questions) and the GHQ-30 (General Health Questionnaire with 30 questions), which measure different aspects of people's health. Moreover, combining information from several variables can improve measurement. For example, rather than asking about household income directly, surveys often use multiple questions asking about different forms of income. This information can then be combined to create a more accurate measure of overall household income.

However, not many surveys have the luxury of asking so many questions on a specific topic and instead will only have space or time to ask a single question such as the standard self-rated health question, 'In general, would you say that your health is excellent, very good, good, fair, or poor?' Here, the subjective nature of the single self-rated health question may make you a bit worried about how the meaning of the question could differ between different people. But on the other hand, plenty of researchers have published leading research papers using the exact same survey question with its inherent weaknesses and biases. As a researcher, it is up to you to decide about the pros and cons of using such a measure.

Moreover, as we mentioned above, the concept of stress is multidimensional. You may be interested in the biological stress response but do not have access to survey data with such biological measurements and so have to make do with survey questions related to stress.

How do your concepts relate

Having decided on your key concepts, questions and measurements, you then need to think about how they relate to each other. From your literature review, you should have some idea about this relationship (or association). The concept that you are trying to explain is usually represented by the **'dependent'** (or **'outcome') variable**, and the **explanatory (or 'independent') variable** represents the factor or factors that explains the dependent variable. It is useful to think of a theory that explains these associations and how one variable (the independent variable) causes another variable (the dependent variable) to occur. Again, from your literature review of the theories and related studies, you may get a good idea which variable is the dependent or the independent variable. However, for other concepts, it may not be possible to put variables within a simple causal framework, and you may need to think of them as correlated variables, or you may need additional concepts and variables in order to bridge the two concepts.

At this stage, it is useful to draw out on a piece of paper the relationship between your concepts and variables. Sometimes it becomes easier to think of relationships between complex concepts by visually representing them on a graph and drawing up lines and causal arrows to relate them together.

Stress → Health

Here, you may be interested in how having a stressful experience affects your health.

Health → Stress

Alternatively, you may be interested in whether having poor health early on in life affects your current levels of stress.

Stress → Biological changes → Health

Here, you may be interested in how stress affects health, perhaps looking at how stress affects people's biology and how this in turn affects their health.

Population and units of analysis

It is really important to think about the population you wish to generalise your research findings to. Most quantitative social science questions look to make inferences beyond the specific data sample, to a wider population. Some secondary data sets have a sampling strategy that makes them claim to be **representative** of subsets of a whole country's population, for example, adults living in private households. Even then, this is not necessarily representative of everyone in the country. In this example, children would be excluded, as would anyone living in an institution (e.g. prison or a care home).

For example, the English Longitudinal Study of Ageing (ELSA) is a longitudinal study of individuals aged 50 years and older who reside in private households in England. When the study began in 2002, it was representative. However, as respondents got older or were lost to follow-up (either through moving out of private residences, death or diminished mental capacity), the sample becomes less representative. The study has accounted for this by adding people (refreshment samples, see section Context of the Study, Chapter 4), at the younger age groups throughout the life of the study.

In some instances, researchers wish to make universal claims that transcend geographical and political boundaries. So they may claim that even though their data was collected from specific types of people living in a particular country, their results can be generalised to other people living in different countries. In the psychological sciences, some of the experimental research done using samples of university students has been written up in terms of inferences to all adults living in all countries. This type of generalisation from a very specific sample may not be appropriate.

Once you decide on the population of your research question, you also need to consider what the unit of analysis is. For a lot of social research, this is an individual person. However, for other researchers such as geographers or demographers, the unit of analysis could be a region or a country.

Chapter Exercises

Specifying your research topic and questions

1   What is your research topic/area? This may be broad to start with and become more refined over time.
2   What are your research question(s)?
3   What are your working hypotheses?

(Continued)

Population and units of analysis

Think about your units of analysis and population and consider the following questions: Do you want your research findings to apply to the population of a country? Which country is this? Or perhaps you are interested in a subpopulation, like the population of children or adults in a particular country. For the units of analysis, is your research question about individuals, households, neighbourhoods, schools, regions or countries? If you want to compare one group to another, remember you will need data on both groups.

Make a note of the units of analysis and population.

Relating your research concepts and measurements

Having developed your research questions and hypotheses, you can start to identify how the concepts and measurements are related to each other:

Your key concepts

Make a list of your key concepts. Some concepts can be quite hard to explain, so practice explaining your research concepts to someone outside of academia.

Now that you have a list of the key concepts in your research, you have an idea of the types of questions, data and variables you will need in a survey.

How do your concepts relate?

It might be useful to identify what are the dependent and independent variables (Figure 2.1). First, think of the dependent variable: the thing you are trying to explain. Then, list the factors you think can help explain your dependent variables.

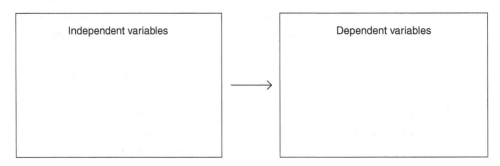

Figure 2.1   Independent and dependent variables

Chapter Summary

- Developing your research questions is often an iterative process.
- Finding your own research topic is something that is often driven by your own interests; once you have decided on a research topic and the related question, you will need to see what data you need in order to answer the research question.

- Having a clear idea of key terms and concepts is very important for working out how they can be measured in your research.
- You will often need to make some difficult choices in terms of the secondary data sets you select.
- Having decided on your key concepts, questions and measurements, you then need to think about how they relate to each other.
- It is fundamental to think about the population you wish to generalise your research findings to. Once you decide on the population of your research question, you also need to consider what the unit of analysis is.

Further Reading

Blaikie, N., & Priest, J. (2019). *Designing social research: The logic of anticipation* (3rd ed.). Polity Press.

3

FINDING SECONDARY DATA

TARANI CHANDOLA

Chapter Overview

Background 22

Your ideal data set 22

Looking for research data 25

Keywords, search terms and databases 28

Practical steps in searching for data 29

Further Reading 32

Background

Once you have a clear idea of your research questions and concepts, you can start searching for suitable data. In this section, you will find information about:

- how to find data for your research project and
- how to evaluate if a particular data set collection is suitable for your research question.

The quantitative data collection in many data archives around the world includes population census, government surveys and other large-scale and/or longitudinal surveys. Some examples of quantitative data sets from around the world include the European Social Survey, the European and World Value Surveys, the Australian Survey of Social Attitudes and the Longitudinal Surveys of Australian Youth in Australia, the Panel Study of Income Dynamics and the Current Population Survey in the USA and Canadian Community Health Survey and the Aboriginal Peoples Survey in Canada. Given the large amounts of data sets that are available through these archives, it can be a bit daunting to try to find the relevant data set for you. These data archives also provide resources to ensure that you are equipped to avoid potential pitfalls in using pre-existing data.

Your ideal data set

Once you decide on your research question or topic, you would normally ask yourself a series of questions to help focus your topic of inquiry. For example, what is the time period you would like covered by the data? Is your research question related to the current time period or historical periods? All archived research data is 'historical', in the sense that the data never reflects the current situation. Some archived data are more 'current' than others, but there is a lag of at least a year before collected data are deposited in archives. This is because the collected data need to go through a process of data cleaning, standardising, documentation, anonymisation and many other procedures before they can be safely released for other people to research. If you are interested in up to the minute data, there are some recent developments in the availability of such data for research purposes. Internet search keyword data on large search engines like Google or Twitter have become very popular sources of data of up to the minute trends and are increasingly used on 'nowcasting' methods – methods that predict the present, the very near future and the very recent past. However, these data from internet search engines have not been gathered for research purposes and are very different from data available from secondary data archives.

Another key question to ask yourself in your search for an ideal data set is what is your main unit of analysis? Are you interested in individuals, countries, businesses or schools? One way of finding out your **unit of analysis** is to think about the relevant unit of analysis for your dependent variable. If you are interested in what makes some people healthier or less stressed compared to other people, then the unit of analysis for your dependent variable is individuals or people. If, however, you want to find out why some regions or countries are healthier than other regions or countries, then your unit of analysis will be regions or countries.

It is also useful to think about what the geographical coverage of your research idea should be. Think of this as what is the wider population you wish to generalise your research to. If you think that your research topic applies to everybody at any period of time, you may wish to analyse research data from multiple countries and societies from multiple periods. However, if you think that your research topic is relevant only to particular societies, communities or groups at a specific point of time, then you will need to find data that is from the same geographical spread as those societies, communities and groups, as well as from the same period. Often, we need to make some compromises when we examine data from different countries and contexts. There may not be any data collected or sampled from exactly the same communities we are interested in, or exactly the same time periods. Indeed, even from within the same survey, the data collection period is not instantaneously occurring at the same time across all contexts and communities. Instead, the data collection period is spread out over time and regions, such that people in some communities may have their data collected in some months (or years) and others have their data collected much later or earlier on.

Do you need a large population representative sample? Ideally, we would all like our data to be representative of the population. For some people, the population means the same thing as all the people in a country, but population could refer to much smaller units such as the population of adults in a country or the population of people in work. When we analyse research data, we nearly always wish to make some inference from the data we analyse back to our population of interest. Hence, having data that is representative of our population of interest is really important. However, for some research questions, such population representation is not so important. For example, if you are interested in the characteristics of a particular community, then you probably do not need to have data from other communities for your research. Many traditional anthropological studies of some communities collected data from all members of that community and did not need to collect data from other types of communities for their research. Their inferences were limited to the specific community they researched.

This brings us to a special type of data collection on all the units within a population – the census. The UK census is a count of all people and households within the country at a particular time. In the UK, census data are collected every 10 years to give us a complete picture of the nation. Apart from questions on who lives at specific addresses, other questions on the age, sex, employment, health and many other characteristics of each person living at a specific address are asked. However, there needs to be a balance between asking lots of questions and the costs of asking those questions (either financial costs or the costs for the people answering those questions). So we cannot find out everything from census data. This is why people run surveys, where they get asked many different types of questions and collect other types of data compared to the census. However, surveys are not censuses, and the compromise is that surveys only represent a small fraction (sample) of the wider population. However, if the surveys are well conducted, then they could be representative of the wider population, allowing you, the researcher, to analyse a wide range of data and make inference back to the population. Both surveys and censuses are available to analyse from the data archives.

How large does a large sample need to be? There is never an easy answer to this question. There are statistical ways of calculating what sample size you need in order to make inference about your research question (see Volume 1 in this series). However, such calculations are rare in secondary data research because they are mainly relevant when you are collecting data (primary data collection) and want to know how many people to sample. As a secondary data analyst, you are limited both by the data collected by the data collectors and the sample size. However, it is still possible to have some rules of thumb about how large a sample size needs to be. For example, if the population you wish to make inference to is in the millions (like the population of a country), then having a sample size of less than 100 people is unlikely to be a good idea. Many survey polls have an average sample size of around 1000 people, from which they infer the voting intentions (and other characteristics) of the country. So having a sample size that is just a couple of hundred units/people when you wish to make inference to the wider population of people in a country is also probably unwise.

What other characteristics do you need for your analysis? Think about your main independent variables and dependent variables. How could your key variables be measured? Here it is useful to see how other researchers have measured the same concepts you are interested in. You can look through the details in the methodology sections of their papers/books. Another way is to look through survey question banks. Usually, we look at survey question banks when we are devising a questionnaire or survey. But these question banks are also useful when we are trying to find secondary data that are relevant to our research questions.

It would be ideal to use surveys or data sets that have valid and reliable measures of the concepts you are interested in. This leads us to the question of what is validity and reliability. The concept of reliability refers to whether you obtain the same answers to your survey question consistently. Consistency can be over time (if you ask someone the same question the next day, will you get the same answer), or across different researchers (if someone else asks the same question, will they get the same answer as you). Validity is the extent to which your question actually measures the concept they are supposed to measure. There are different types of measures of validity, but the most common are face validity (the question appears 'on its face' to measure the concept of interest), content validity (your question 'covers' different aspects of the concept of interest) and criterion validity (the extent to which answers to the question are correlated with other questions they are meant to be correlated with).

It is not easy to 'prove' that a particular variable or survey question is reliable and valid, we often have to rely on existing research to show this or conduct a separate piece of research to show this. That is why, where it is possible, it is a much better idea to use measures and questions that have already been shown to be valid and reliable measures of the concepts you are interested in. How can you know whether the question is valid or reliable? You can look through existing question banks like the survey question bank. If a particular question has been used in a well-known and respected survey, it is likely that the survey designers have gone through a process of making sure that the question is valid and reliable. You will still need to check the underpinning research that there has been some validity or reliability studies on that particular question, but having the same question asked repeatedly in different surveys gives you some confidence that the question may be a valid and reliable way of measuring the concept you are interested in.

There are many different survey question banks that can be accessed through this link: www.ukdataservice.ac.uk/get-data/other-providers/question-banks.

It is useful to explore these question banks using keywords to get some sense of how questions have been asked in different surveys. However, if you are new to a field, you may not know all the relevant keywords. Further in this chapter, we describe some of the online resources such as a thesaurus for research keywords that could help in your search for relevant survey questions.

Looking for research data

Starting your search for research data

Where should we be looking for data? Nowadays, most people search the internet using an internet search engine. However, common search engines are not really well set up to search for research data. Instead, it may be more useful to search specialist websites that specialise in archiving research data.

But before we explore some of these digital data archives, it is worth exploring other ways of obtaining research data.

It is really important to read key papers or books on the topic you are interested in and use those papers/books to find out what data has been used for in that piece of research. How do you know if it is a key paper? Citations are usually a good indicator – the greater the number of citations, the more likely that paper or book will be a key resource. Within those key papers or books you have identified, if it is a good paper with the methodology well documented, then the data sources should be named and listed, as well as how to access the data. Digital data sets now have digital object identifiers (DOIs) which are hyperlinked permanent web addresses. Just like DOIs for journal papers, DOIs are also created for data sets and associated outputs. DOIs are a permanent identifier which links to data sets that can be persistently accessed, which have been curated and have rich metadata. This also enables accurate data citation and bibliometrics.

Some of the archived data sources will have a paper dedicated to describing the data, which will include instructions on how to access the data. For example, several longitudinal cohort studies are profiled in the *International Journal of Epidemiology*. Nowadays, many research grant funders specify that in order to obtain funding for data collection, data collectors need to make this data available for other researchers to use. Some of these data will be made available through a data archive. For other data sets, availability can be through a bespoke website. You will need to fill in some details, but the data can be made available for verified researchers after a screening process by the data collectors. If you cannot find any data access website, you could just email the researchers directly and ask if they are willing to share the data.

Search tool 1: Searching for a particular data set within the UKDS

Identify and make a note of the names of the surveys or data sets you already know. These are data sets that may have been mentioned by previous studies or textbooks, or they may have been identified in the news. Once you know the name of the data set, you can try to find it in data archives like the UKDS.

- Go to http://ukdataservice.ac.uk
- Type in the name of the data set you have identified in the <Search Data> box.

When you enter terms you want to search for, such as 'health', or 'energy prices', a list with strings and keywords will appear while you are typing.

Search tool 2: Key data within the UKDS

One of the easiest ways to find data is by clicking on the 'Key data' tab of the UKDS. The key data pages highlight the most popular data sets within that data archive. These data sets are grouped by tabs for different types of data, such as UK surveys, cross-national surveys, longitudinal studies, international macrodata, census data, business microdata and qualitative/mixed methods. Browsing the names and descriptions of these key data sources is a useful way of finding high-quality data.

- Go to http://ukdataservice.ac.uk > Get data > Key data.
- If you are looking for cross-national or longitudinal data, select the relevant tab.

Make a note of any data sets that seem relevant to your research question.

Search tool 3: Theme pages within the UKDS

The theme pages list data available for research into a number of key themes, including crime, health and housing. Theme pages also include advice, research examples and links to relevant resources.

- Go to http://ukdataservice.ac.uk > Get data > Data by theme.
- Is there a relevant theme for your research?
- If so, do the pages highlight any relevant data sources?

Search tool 4: The UKDS data catalogue

Another way to access data is to use the UKDS Data Catalogue search engine. To use the Data Catalogue, you need to identify relevant search terms such as keywords.

- Go to http://ukdataservice.ac.uk > Get data.
- Type in your search term and press 'go'.

When using the search engine, remember the following:

- Spaces between words are interpreted as AND by default.
- You can also use the Boolean operators OR or NOT for complex searches.

What happens if you get too many results?

The UKDS catalogue contains a lot of data. Therefore, your search is likely to produce an unhelpfully large number of results. This means an important part of using the catalogue is finding ways to narrow your search. When searching for a data collection, you can narrow your search based on other characteristics. These include the following:

Data: Limit your search to data relevant to a particular period.

Topic: Narrow your search using a predefined list of topics.

Data type: Choose between cross-sectional surveys, longitudinal data, qualitative data and more.

Access: Data can be safeguarded, open or controlled. Open data sets are usually ready for you to download, so long as you are registered as a researcher belonging to a university. Safeguarded or controlled data usually requires additional forms of checking for your research credentials and can take a few days or longer for you to be given access to the data.

Country: Pick a geographical location that is relevant to your question.

You can sort your results by choosing a sorting order: most recently published studies, relevance, alphabetical order of the titles and reversed alphabetical order of the titles. Relevance is probably the most useful criteria to sort your results by.

For further details on a particular data set, click on the title of a study. This brings you to the 'Data Catalogue' record which contains very detailed information (in the 'Details' tab) about the Title, Study number (SN), PID, Series, Principal investigator(s), Sponsors and contributors, Topics, Abstract, Citation and copyright, Edition history. The Data Catalogue record also contains information about the documentation, the resources and access conditions.

Who can access the data?

Researchers, students and teachers from any discipline, organisation or country may register with the UKDS and obtain data. However, there may be some restrictions on accessing them in the UKDS due to the licence agreements the UKDS have with the data providers. If you are from a commercial organisation, there are further restrictions on accessing the data.

Keywords, search terms and databases

When you are looking for data, it is always a good idea to have some idea about keywords and standard search terms that are used in research literature. This is because you can often end up with thousands of hits that may not be relevant to your research question, and it is very inefficient to go through all those hits when you could have done a more efficient search resulting in more relevant (and fewer) hits.

Let us take a common word like 'stress', and you want to search for data on the topic. It is possible to search for data on that particular word. However, be prepared for the thousands of hits on the word 'stress' from the UKDS question bank and more than 300 hits if you search for 'stress' on the data they hold on that data archive (www.ukdataservice.ac.uk).

Another way to look for data is through standard keyword searches on the HASSET multidisciplinary thesaurus database (https://hasset.ukdataservice.ac.uk). The Humanities and Social Science Electronic Thesaurus (HASSET) is the leading British English thesaurus for the social sciences. HASSET has been compiled at the UK Data Archive for over 30 years. It was developed initially as an information retrieval tool to access data deposited in the UK Data Archive. Its scope has now expanded to cover the collections held by the UKDS.

Entering 'stress' as a keyword on the HASSET database results in two hits for the term – one is 'STRESS (PSYCHOLOGICAL)' and the other is 'POST-TRAUMATIC STRESS DISORDER'. If we are interested in the former concept, we can click through, and this gives us the HASSET thesaurus concept webpage that locates stress within the hierarchy of psychological effects, which also contains terms such as *anxiety*, *depression*, *phobias* and *trauma*. This webpage also gives us a link to search the Data Catalogue for entries related to the keyword. Clicking on that link then gives us 254 results for studies related to stress.

However, stress means different things to different people. So searching for 'stress' may not be as useful as searching for particular words you would expect to find in a survey question about stress. People who design survey questions try to avoid confusing terms that could mean different things to different people. So perhaps it may be a good idea not to directly search for the word 'stress' in a survey question. On the other hand, what other words could you search for in a survey question if you are interested in the topic of stress?

We could note that the concepts of anxiety and depression are closely related to stress – we could search for those terms instead. However, they also could have very specific meanings, such as to have a clinical diagnosis of anxiety or depression. It is worth looking at a general thesaurus for synonyms of stress. Here we find quite a few candidates, including 'worry'.

Practical steps in searching for data

Let us imagine that you are interested in the topic of work stress with an underlying question about who has more work stress. Is it bosses at the top who are more stressed about work than the employees at the bottom of the company hierarchy? How will you go about searching for secondary data on the topic?

First of all, you will need to review the literature on the social distribution of work stress to find out if this question has already been answered. It may be that there may be limitations in existing studies that prompt you to go further than what has already been done and published. So you then need to find what secondary data there are on the topic of work stress. If you find out the names of the data sets that studies have used to publish on the topic of work stress, you can then search for whether those data sets are available through portals such as the UKDS or through other data access websites.

Another approach is to do keyword search terms for work stress in data search engines such as on the UKDS. You can enter the term *work stress* into a search field for data on the UKDS website (www.ukdataservice.ac.uk/get-data). Remember to use the quotations around the search term, otherwise you will get search findings that relate to both work and stress, not just for 'work stress'. This currently results in three hits – the Health Survey for England (HSE), 1993; the Adult Psychiatric Morbidity Survey, 2007; and the Special License access for the Adult Psychiatric Morbidity Survey, 2014. You then need to click on each of these hits. Three hits for data on 'work stress' are probably too low, as work stress is a common research topic, and there should be other secondary data available on the topic. This particular data search strategy has resulted in too few hits.

Thankfully, there are easy ways to expand the search to a broader keyword if your keyword search has resulted in too few data sets being identified. If you click through on the 'details' tab of one of the three studies (e.g. the HSE, 1993), you can discover the thesaurus keyword terms associated with each data set. Reading through all the keyword terms, you can discover other keywords that may be of relevance. For example, 'job satisfaction' appears as one of the keywords for the HSE, 1993, data set. Clicking on that keyword gets you to the HASSET thesaurus search concept page linked to that keyword. On this page, there are suggestions for broader keyword terms such as 'working conditions'. There is also a link there to 'search in data catalogue' and clicking on that link results in 354 secondary data sets with measures of 'working conditions'. Now clicking on each data set and reading about 354 data sets will take too long, so it is probably a good idea to find ways of narrowing down that list of data sets to something more manageable, such as refining the search in terms of particular features of the data you are interested in. For example, you can look for particular topic areas. If you are interested in the social distribution of work stress, it may be that you choose 'social stratification and groupings' as the topic area, and this narrows down the list to 99 data sets. Or it might be that you are interested in particular types of data such as cohort and longitudinal studies, which would also narrow down the list of data sets.

It would be very time-consuming to go through all these hits to find the data and questions that are relevant to you. This process could be quite laborious to click on each data set and go through all the documentation associated with the data sets you find to find out whether they have got particular questions measured. Thankfully, there are other ways to search for data, especially the specific questions that are asked in secondary data. This is through the Nesstar website (http://nesstar.ukdata service.ac.uk/webview). Here you can enter a visual data library where you can search, browse and download a selected range of key social and economic data available on the UKDS website.

If you type 'work stress' into the search box of the UKDS Nesstar website, you will actually get no hits. However, if you enter the search term 'stress', you will get lots of hits on data sets with some measures of stress. Searching on the Nesstar website allows you to have a look at the specific question that was asked in a study and also gives you the distribution of responses to that particular question. This can really help in narrowing down your search from hundreds of potential data sets to just a handful of data sets that have the specific questions you would like to examine.

Another way to search for data sets is using the UKDS variable and question bank, which allows you to search and browse variables and questions from survey data sets.

Go to the UKDS variable and question bank (https://discover.ukdataservice.ac.uk/variables).

Search for the term 'work stress', and you will get 54 results. A lot of the results are about medications people may take to deal with their work stress, primarily from the Adult Psychiatric Morbidity Survey, 2007. The same survey also contains questions from two questionnaires about work stressors – the Effort–Reward Imbalance model and the Job Content Questionnaire. As both models are well-known and validated models of work stress, it would be useful to investigate more data sets that contain these questions.

Chapter Summary

- The quantitative data collection in many data archives around the world includes population census, government surveys and other large-scale and/or longitudinal surveys.
- Once you decide on your research question or topic, you would normally ask yourself a series of questions to help focus your topic of inquiry. For example, What is the time period you would like covered by the data? What is your main unit of analysis? Do you need a large population representative sample?
- Try to use surveys or data sets that have valid and reliable measures of the concepts you are interested in.

(Continued)

- It is really important to read key papers or books on the topic you are interested in and use those papers/books to find out what data has been used in that piece of research.
- Once you know the name of the data set, you can try to find it in data archives like the UKDS, HASSET and Nesstar.
- When you are looking for data, it is always a good idea to have some idea about keywords and standard search terms that are used in research literature.

Further Reading

Cole, K., Wathan, J., & Corti, L. (2008). The provision of access to quantitative data for secondary analysis. In N. Fielding, R. M. Lee, & G. Blank (Eds.), *The SAGE handbook of online research methods* (pp. 364–384). Sage.

Goodwin, J. (2012b). Sage secondary data analysis: Vol. IV. Ethical, methodological and practical issues in secondary analysis. Sage.

Kiecolt, K., & Nathan, L. (1985). *Secondary analysis of survey data*. Sage.

4

GETTING TO KNOW THE DATA

TARANI CHANDOLA

Chapter Overview

Background 34

Interpreting data correctly 34

Using nesstar to explore data 42

Further Reading 45

Background

Congratulations – you have found your data. What should you do first? Dive into data? Read metadata documents? Read research papers? This is an iterative process. Let us assume that you have finalised your research question, and you have some idea of the variables you wish to investigate.

The next step is to find out if you can access the data. If the data is from an online data archive, you will need to register with the data archive. Most of the data available in online archives is available to all researchers, but each data catalogue record contains a statement about 'access conditions' – telling you whether there are any restrictions in accessing a specific data set. So it is wise not to dive straight into the questionnaire or variable list of a specific data set, without first finding out if you can access the data.

Once you find out that you can access the data, you need to discover if it contains measures of all the concepts you are interested in and what those specific variables are. How do you find out? You do this by reading through the reports from the primary data collectors and reading through the questionnaires, the metadata and the technical reports. That is a lot of reading to do, and it can be very daunting at first, so this chapter helps you with the steps you need to carry out to get to know the data.

Interpreting data correctly

Users of secondary data are seldom involved in the data collection process, so you will need to spend some time exploring associated documentation. This will help you understand how the data was collected, from whom it was collected and what was done with it after data collection.

Evaluating the data catalogue entry

When you are trying to understand a secondary data set, most of the time, you as the researcher will not have an in-depth insider understanding about the data that someone who collected the data does. This means you need to spend quite a bit of time getting to know the data set well and especially reading through the documentation provided with the data set. You should also always try to have a critical understanding of the data. This means being aware of any limitations in the study design that resulted in the data being collected and also being aware of how suitable the data is for your own research purposes, such as whether or not the data that was collected is suitable for your research questions.

Emma Smith (2008) provides an excellent list of issues to think about when approaching a data set to reanalyse it. The following is based on the questions she asks analysts to consider once the research aims have been established:

- How was the data collected? We would place greater trust in the data collected by a reputable organisation such as a commercial survey research agency or academic institution with trained staff. This is because those organisations tend to use more robust and objective procedures for data collection and also to document their data collection procedures properly. This should give you greater confidence in the reuse of data deposited by these organisations. Most data that is deposited in the data archives would be from such reputable organisations, although it is still important to check their credentials before using their data.
- What types of questions were used? Do the questions appear to be unbiased and easy to answer? How reliable are the questions – will people give the same answer if you gave them the same question again? Most of the data sets from data archives have a copy of the data collection instrument (most commonly a survey questionnaire or interview schedule) in the documentation. You will need to examine the 'face validity' of the questions, and for any specific questions you are interested in, examine whether there are existing studies that establish the validity and reliability of those questions to measure your concept of interest in the sampled population.
- How relevant are the data to your own research question? You need to check the data documentation to see if the data contain the right topics for your research question. Even though your research topic of interest is covered in a data set, it may be that the specific questions you are interested in were not asked in the survey. You need to check the questions asked in the questionnaire and any other related data documentation, such as how some summary of variables were derived.
- What are the sampling strategies and response rates? It is common for most statistical methods on survey data to assume that data collected is representative of the population and that individual units (people) are sampled at random. However, in reality, most data sets are not from a simple random survey and instead from more complex of sampling procedures. This will get you to use particular analytical techniques to adjust for this. The sample size of the data is a critical issue. Many secondary data sets may have too small a sample size to carry out meaningful analyses. For example, you may be able to describe associations between feelings of stress and social class in a sample size of 100 people, but once you start taking account of all the factors that can cause an association between class and stress (e.g. health, personality factors, age, cultural factors), you will quickly run up against problems of small sample sizes.
- Who was in the population from which the sample was drawn? For example, it may be that your sample reflects different but overlapping populations. The 2011 UK census is meant to represent all individuals living in the UK in 2011. In contrast, many surveys are representative of people (often adults) living in private households. The geographical reach is also important, with many people making incorrect inferences to the UK population, when the survey was conducted in England.

- Are there missing values? **Missing values** are a key concern in any data analysis as there may be several reasons for why the data are missing. It is possible that some people did not understand the question, or preferred not to answer the question. Or it may be that there was a mistake in the way the questionnaire was written, and people were not asked a question when they were meant to be asked. Reasons for substantial amounts of missing data should always be investigated.

Establishing the coverage, universe and methodology of the data

Online resources on the methodology of data sets

The data provided by cross-sectional and longitudinal studies can cover a multitude of topics, including education, employment, health, income, family and social networks. These data are valuable resources which allow researchers to understand how changes in these topics have effects on the circumstances of an individual's life in the short, middle and long term.

There are several resources for learning about the information contained in different cross-sectional and longitudinal data sets. The CLOSER Learning Hub (https://learning.closer.ac.uk) and the UKDS Nesstar Catalogue (http://nesstar.ukdataservice.ac.uk/webview) allow for exploration of data included across several data sets. Information on individual data sets can often be found on their websites, more specifically in their user guides, **codebooks** and data documentation.

Context of the study

Whether you choose to use **cross-sectional data**, data collected from individuals once, **longitudinal data** or data collected repeatedly from the same individuals over time, it is important to understand the context of the data and the implications for interpretation of the findings. Cross-sectional data can only show associations between variables; however, you cannot infer anything about temporality or causation. By using longitudinal data, you can get an understanding of how people's circumstances change over time, and through the use of data analysis, you can begin to infer causality.

Cross-sectional data are collected from individuals once, although some studies collect cross-sectional data multiple times, for example, the Labour Force Survey (LFS) or the HSE. These repeated cross-sectional data are what many researchers and government departments use to establish trends. Longitudinal studies, on the other hand, collect data from the same people repeatedly. Some longitudinal studies collect data from cohorts of individuals, for example, the 1970 British Cohort Study, the Millennium Cohort Study (MCS) and the National Child Development Study (NCDS) are all examples of birth cohort studies. Other types of longitudinal studies include panel studies such as the British Household Panel Survey (BHPS), Understanding Society (UK Household Longitudinal Study [UKHLS]) and the ONS Longitudinal Study (ONS LS). Panel studies recruit a group of individuals and follow them over a period of time at regular intervals. The BHPS and UKHLS collect data annually, whereas the ONS LS collects data every 10 years.

The unit of data collection must also be taken into account when determining the context of a study. The individual is usually the unit of data collection for studies; however, households can also be the unit of data collection, for example, BHPS and UKHLS. The use of households as the unit of data collection allows for the investigation of inter-relationships between individuals in the household.

Examples of other contextual factors include country or region, age, gender or ethnicity. Some studies will oversample respondents in these categories in order to be able to conduct subsample analysis of the data.

Sample attrition and changing sample characteristics may require recruitment of additional individuals into a study. These boost or refreshment samples maybe added at any time during the duration of the study. The UKHLS has had one boost sample, the Immigrant and Ethnic Minority Boost. This boost was used to add new immigrant and ethnic minorities to the study to better represent the changing UK population. The ELSA has had four refreshment samples which have recruited 50- to 51-year-olds to maintain a sample that is 50 years and older.

Accessing the data

Many data sets can be accessed through the UKDS, other data sets may only be accessed through the managing institution. Some data can be accessed through a standard end user licence. Other more restricted data, such as educational records, neighbourhood-level data or biological or genetic data, may require additional limits be put on the access of the data and may require an application for access or use of the data.

Researchers, students and teachers from any discipline, organisation or country may register with the UKDS and obtain data. However, some data sets have restrictions on access due to licence agreements. There are three types of licences. Data licensed for use with an 'open licence' are data which are not personal and have relatively few restrictions to use. You do not need to login or register for using these data and can access and download the data directly. Data licensed for use in the 'safeguarded' category are not personal data, but there is a risk of disclosing personal information if these data are linked to other data sets. Controlled data are data which could allow the individual data subjects to be identified. These data are only available to users who have been accredited and their data usage has been approved by the relevant Data Access Committee. Safeguarded and controlled data require registration/authentication.

Most of the example data sets we use in this book are in the safeguarded category, so this will require you to register with the UKDS. If you are from a UK institution of higher or further education or your organisation is on this list of federation members (www.ukfederation.org.uk/content/Documents/AccountableIdPs), you do not need to register but can log in to the UKDS using your local username and password. If you are from an organisation not using federated access management, you will need to register your details and complete a form to request a username (https://beta.ukdata service.ac.uk/myaccount/credentials).

Data can be delivered through a variety of media. Most data available through the UKDS can be downloaded in compressed folders. Other data may only be accessed through secure rooms or may be delivered on physical drives such as USB sticks or CDs. It is necessary to be familiar with the licence agreements of all secondary data you use. Some data should not be stored on computers with access to the internet, sharing of data with other researchers may not be permitted unless stated on the contract or application, and some data must be destroyed after the project has been completed and any physical drives may need to be destroyed or sent back to the managing institution.

Data can be delivered in a variety of formats which allows for direct input into statistical programs. These include **SAS**, **STATA**, **SPSS** and tab formats. You can often choose which format you wish to access prior to receiving the data.

Data structure

The data structures will be explained in the data documentation of each study. Depending on the structure and complexity of the data, you may receive one file or several data files. The National Child Development Study provides one data file per wave of data collection; conversely the UKHLS has several data files per wave of data collection. Both repeated cross-sectional and longitudinal studies may have file naming conventions which indicate the time period or wave of data collection. The LFS uses a system which indicates the quarter_year of data collection. UKHLS and the BHPS use letters to indicate the waves of data collection, while UKHLS uses a letter_filename convention, the BHPS just uses letterfilename.

Some data files will include data from a specific unit, that is, individuals or households. Other files may contain information that was only collected on or from a subset of respondents – that is, births, employment histories, youth and so on.

Within each data file will be a variable or number of variables that can be used to identify the units of observation of the study. Household studies may have both a household identifier, a person identifier and a head of household identifier. Cross-sectional studies may have an individual identifier, while longitudinal studies may have longitudinal identifier, often an individual identifier.

Variable names and conventions

Studies often have different variable naming conventions, and these conventions may change over the course of the study, in the case of longitudinal studies. As data has become more widely accessible, naming conventions have become more user friendly; however, it is important to read data documentation to understand how variable names may have changed between data collection waves or among different samples in the same data collection wave. Some studies use prefixes or suffixes to indicate the sample who received those specific questions, while others may put these questions in a separate data file with no special identifiers. In these cases, you may need to rename these variables prior to merging with other data sets with the same names as you will overwrite the data.

As noted, some individuals may answer a specific set of questions while others don't. For example, only people currently working may answer job stress-related questions, while non-working people will not. Thus, it is important to know the 'universe' of people who have answered specific questions. This is another area where data documentation will tell you who answered one or a group of questions. Questionnaires may also provide information on who answered certain questions. Some studies allow proxy responses, that is, someone who knows the person the questions are being asked about answers those questions. Often there is an indicator when **proxy respondents** are used, and missing code values may also include 'proxy' when questions are not asked of proxy respondents.

While studies endeavour to get respondents to answer all questions, there may be some questions which remain unanswered. There are various reasons for having missing data, and often studies create codes which indicate potential reasons for missingness. In the example of job stress, the questions may include a 'not applicable' code which would apply to those not currently in work. User guides, codebooks and data documentation will describe the missing code values used. Sometimes missing codes are added due to the addition of refreshment or boost samples or inclusion of new variables, so it is important to familiarise yourself with these in every new release of data.

Studies will often provide a number of variables that are either a combination of variables or are reduced versions of variables. These derived variables may also come with their own naming conventions. **Derived variables** are often commonly used, and by using these variables, researchers may have increased confidence when comparing their findings to others who use the same variables. Some examples of derived variables are gross or net individual income, Short Form-12 Physical or Mental Component Score, educational qualifications and social class. A list of derived variables may be listed in user guides, additionally data documentation may list the variables used to derive specific variables.

Key variables

Most studies have key variables which can be used to identify the unit of analysis or to link units longitudinally. Most studies have an individual identifier which will identify a person or a single unit. Some studies nest single units in larger units, that is, households, schools, regions and so on; thus, studies will also include an identifier for these units as well. Other key variables may indicate subsamples of respondents, that is, boost or refreshment, region, age, gender and so on.

Exploring the survey documentation

Typically, when you click on a particular data set in the UK Data Archive, you get details such as the title of the data set, the DOI of the data set, whether it belongs to a data series, who deposited the data and who the Principal Investigators (or PIs) were, who the data collectors were and who the funders (sponsors) of that data collection were. Why is the source of funding for the data important for a secondary researcher? For some studies, you may be dubious if the data were funded by particular interest groups who may try to influence the quality of the data collected. Usually, data funded by research council-funded studies are of high quality, so that gives you, the secondary data researcher, some reassurance about the quality of the data set.

There are a number of additional details listed that describe the data set. For example, the citation details are important because you need to know how to cite the data if you use it. The subject categories tell you some of the general and most important topics covered in the data, which are summarised in the abstract. The coverage, universe and methodology provide summary details of the sampling strategy and the sample population. Details about the dates and spatial locations of the fieldwork are important so that you know what period and spatial contexts the data relate to. Also, the units of sampling will tell you whether this is an individual-, household- or area-level data set. The type of data will be described, whether they are cross-sectional or longitudinal data. The sampling process will also be described, whether some type of random sampling was used – this is important for knowing whether the sample can be generalised to a wider population. A critical piece of information is the number of **cases**, which is the sample size of the data. Ideally, you would like the data to have a large sample size as that has better statistical properties than a small sample size. The data description will also tell you whether the data were collected by questionnaire or face-to-face interview.

The data documentation will usually include the questionnaire, a technical report and the read file containing the different formats the data is available in. The survey technical report will describe the sampling, achieved sample size, fieldwork and weighting of the data. The level of detail may vary depending on the scale and resourcing of the survey. There may be additional documents such as information leaflets and showcards for participants and forms for obtaining their consent.

A key piece of documentation is the questionnaire or interview schedule. This is perhaps the first large document that is useful to read, as it describes all the questions that were asked in the study and the sequence of those questions. It is usually a good idea to read through the whole questionnaire. This gives you an idea about the different topics covered by the questionnaire and also about the context of the data. For example, is it a short or long questionnaire, or how burdensome was the survey or questionnaire for the interviewee? Furthermore, some survey questionnaires are not straightforward to follow and have complex routings between questions. It is not so obvious when some questions get asked and in which order.

Sometimes it is better to print out the questionnaire and make notes on particular topics and questions you are interested in. However, some of the questionnaires can be very long, more than 100 pages, so in order to save trees and printing costs, it is worth making digital notes on the pdf questionnaires. Also, you should make notes of particular questions. Sometimes the variable names are displayed next to the question, which makes it easier for you to find those questions in the data set.

A useful exercise is to complete the questionnaire as though you are the respondent. This gives you an idea about how easy or tough it is to answer the questions, how valid those questions are and how long it takes to do the survey.

The documentation will also contain instructions of the interviewers, if the data were collected by interviews. If these instructions are commercially sensitive, then a summary of briefing content, coding frames and coding instructions provided to the interviewers should be provided.

There should also be links to primary reports and publications by the original data collectors. There may also be some documentation about whether some questionnaire variables may have been removed from the deposited data and the reason for this (e.g. to protect the privacy of individuals in the study). Information about any known errors or issues in the data should also be documented. Sometimes derived variable specifications are also available – these are another very useful source of information about the study and are extremely useful for a secondary data analyst.

Using Nesstar to explore data

You don't need to download the data first, or even get permissions. Some of the data can be explored from your web browser:

www.ukdataservice.ac.uk/get-data/explore-online

Nesstar is the online data exploration system used by the UKDS to provide access to a wide variety of data sets. All visitors to the Nesstar Catalogue can browse study metadata and variable frequencies and use the simple and advanced search options. Registered users can also create simple online cross tabulations, produce graphs and download subsets of variables in a variety of formats.

Note: Not all UKDS data sets are available to explore online via Nesstar.

Clicking on http://nesstar.ukdataservice.ac.uk/webview takes you to the Nesstar home page. At the top left-hand side of the page, there is a search box with a magnifying glass (for a simple search) and another magnifying glass with a '+' image for more advanced searches.

Below the search box, there are three types of data sets listed – research data sets, unrestricted access data sets and teaching data sets.

It would be useful to first register with Nesstar so that you can use all the functionalities of the website and access the research and teaching data sets. However, in this example, we will use some data from the unrestricted access data sets list to show the basic functions of the website.

Clicking on unrestricted access data sets and then on unrestricted access – research data sets, you are presented with a list of five data sets. Given that we have defined our area of interest to be work stress, perhaps the most promising of the data sets could be the European Quality of Life Survey. Clicking on that survey leads to an open access version of the European Quality of Life Survey Time Series, 2007 and 2011, with two rows below for the metadata and variable description (Figure 4.1). Click on the variable description tab, and let's select the most recent data set (2011), and once within, select variables related to subjective well-being. Looking through the long list of variables in that survey related to subjective well-being, we find one question, 'How satisfied are you with: Your present job?' Clicking on that reveals the distribution of that variable in the right-hand side of the browser. The question has 10 categories with survey respondents choosing from 1 (very dissatisfied) to 10 (very satisfied). This is a Likert-type scale. You can also see a histogram of the distribution and can tell that this is not a normally distributed variable, but instead a variable that is highly skewed to the left, as most people report being satisfied with their work and relatively few people are at the dissatisfied end at the left-hand side of the distribution (towards 1).

Figure 4.1 Screenshot from the UK Data Service Nesstar resource on the distribution of 'How satisfied are you with: Your present job?' from the data Set European Quality of Life Time Series, 2011

You can also explore how this variable is associated with other characteristics of the survey respondent. Click on the Tabulation tab next to the Description tab towards the top of the right-hand side panel of the web browser. This will show a table where you can choose to add selected variables to the row or column. If you go back to the 'How satisfied are you with your job' question on the left-hand side and click that again, you now get an option to add this to a row or column.

Before choosing between rows and columns, it is useful to think of whether the variables you are analysing are dependent or independent variables. It is often useful to have dependent variables as rows and independent variables as columns. Think of this as a graphical way of presenting your results. In a graph, the *x*-axis is usually the independent variable and the *y*-axis the dependent variable. If we look at a table, the *y*-axis represents the rows (each unit on the *y*-axis corresponds to a row on each variable). Similarly, the *x*-axis represents the columns (each unit on the *x*-axis corresponds to a category of the independent variable.

So choose 'add to row', and you will see the distribution of this variable once again on the right-hand panel, but this time it is displayed as a table without the histogram. Now you need to think of the variable to add in as a column. This could be something you think should predict the levels of work satisfaction or dissatisfaction. We had an idea of investigating the question of whether people at the top of the socio-economic ladder are more stressed. If this was true, we would see rich people reporting higher levels of dissatisfaction than poor people. We can explore this hypothesis by finding an appropriate question from the variable list that measures how rich or poor someone is. Have a look at the questions under the heading 'economic situation of household'. There you can see quite a few variables on household income and affordability. One of the questions is 'Thinking of your household's total monthly income: Is your household able to make ends meet?' (Figure 4.2). Clicking on this question and adding it to the table as a column will result in a table where the columns represent the household income variable and the rows represent the job dissatisfaction variable. By default, the table displays column percentages, but this can be changed to the row numbers or the row percentages using the drop-down box towards the top. Actually, column percentages work well for the question, because looking at the figures, they reveal the percentage of respondents within each household monthly income category with different levels of job satisfaction. Towards the top of the rows, we have people who are very dissatisfied with their job (scoring 1), and we see that as we go from the left-hand column (very easily make ends meet) to the right-hand columns (great difficulty in making ends meet), there is an increase in the percentages. There is almost a 10-fold difference in the percentage of respondents who report they can easily make ends meet and are also very dissatisfied with their job (0.9%) and the percentage of respondents who report they make ends meet with great difficulty and

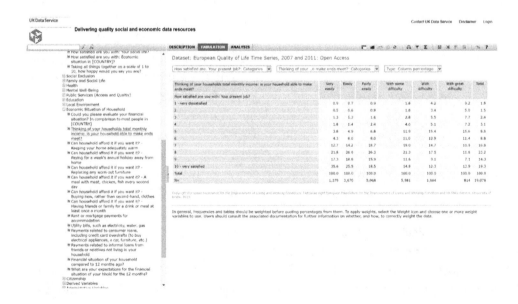

Figure 4.2 Screenshot from the UK Data Service Nesstar resource on the cross tabulation of 'How satisfied are you with: Your present job?' by 'Is your household able to make ends meet?' from the data Set European Quality of Life Time Series, 2011

are also very dissatisfied with their job (9.2%). Levels of job satisfaction appear to be affected by household finances.

What would happen if we chose row percentages? The meaning of the table would change. Instead of describing the differences in job satisfaction between household finance groups, we would be describing the differences in household finance between job satisfaction levels. Only 3.6% of participants who are very dissatisfied with their present job can make ends meet very easily. In contrast 13.3% of participants who are very satisfied with their present job can make ends meet easily. Making ends meet appears to be affected by levels of job satisfaction.

Chapter Summary

- Most of the data available in online archives are available to all researchers, but check their 'access conditions' statement to see if there are any restrictions.
- Users of secondary data are seldom involved in the data collection process, so you will need to spend some time exploring the associated documentation.
- Smith (2008) provides a handy list of questions to think about when evaluating a data set:
  - How were the data collected?
  - What types of questions were used?
  - How relevant are the data to your own research question?
  - What are the sampling strategies and response rates?
  - Who was in the population from which the sample was drawn?
  - Are there missing values?
- There are several resources for learning about the information contained in different cross-sectional and longitudinal data sets. The CLOSER Learning Hub (https://learning. closer.ac.uk) and the UKDS Nesstar Catalogue (http://nesstar.ukdataservice.ac.uk/ webview) allow for exploration of data included across several data sets.
- It is important to understand the context of the data and the implications for interpretation of the findings.
- The unit of data collection and other contextual factors such as country or region, age, gender or ethnicity should also be taken into consideration.
- Studies often have different variable naming conventions, and these conventions may change over the course of the study, in the case of longitudinal studies.
- Most studies have key variables which can be used to identify the unit of analysis or to link units longitudinally.

Further Reading

Lynn, P. (2016). Principles of sampling. In T. Greenfield & S. Greener (Eds.), *Research methods for postgraduates* (3rd ed., pp. 244–254). Wiley.

5

BASIC DATA MANAGEMENT

CARA BOOKER

Chapter Overview

Background 48

Basic data manipulation commands in the statistical software
packages SPSS and stata 48

Building a usable data set 50

Common problems with getting familiar with secondary data sets 52

Tips on handling secondary data sets 53

Getting to know the understanding society data set 57

Practical exercise 63

Further Reading 67

Background

Following on from the research question we used in the earlier chapters (Who is more stressed at work?) and the data we found using the UKDS data search tools, we will use Understanding Society (UKHLS) and the ELSA as data examples. These are complex data sets, with many waves of data and with different levels of data, but it is very useful to explore and understand some of the complexities.

The Understanding Society (UKHLS) data sets can be accessed from UKDS through this link: https://beta.ukdataservice.ac.uk/datacatalogue/series/series?id=2000053, and the ELSA data sets through this link: https://beta.ukdataservice.ac.uk/datacatalogue/series/series?id=200011. Alternatively, you can type in the names of those data sets in the UKDS search data catalogue form on the home page of the UKDS (www.ukdataservice.ac.uk).

Data from data archives will often come in various formats for use in different statistical software packages such as SPSS, STATA or SAS. In addition, there should be an option for getting the data in text format, which can be read by all software packages. Text data imported into a statistics package needs additional information telling the software what the variable names are and other details about the data. For simplicity, we will be using examples about data management with SPSS and STATA, which are the standard formats that secondary data from the UKDS makes available for downloads.

Basic data manipulation commands in the statistical software packages SPSS and STATA

Using a syntax or command file

Although both SPSS and STATA have windows point and click buttons, through which you can do a lot of data manipulations and statistical analyses, it is highly advisable for any secondary data researcher to become familiar with some of the basic commands in these statistical packages which are used in their programming or command-driven windows interface. This is because of a number of reasons. You will easily get tired of pointing and clicking in a windows interface, especially when you have to repeatedly do the same actions over and over again. Furthermore, when you are repeating commands, it is much easier to copy and paste those commands into the command interface, rather than pointing and clicking repeatedly. Moreover, saving the command interface means that you have a record of what data manipulations and statistical analysis you have done. When you need to go back to analyses you have previously done, this record is invaluable. All too often, if you do not have this record of the commands you have used, you will forget what you have previously done.

This chapter will concentrate on SPSS and STATA commands – the two most common file formats available in UKDS.

For further details on some introductory and basic commands, here are some useful websites:

SPSS: https://stats.idre.ucla.edu/spss/seminars/introduction-to-spss-syntax-2

STATA: https://stats.idre.ucla.edu/stata/faq/how-do-i-do-this-spss-command-in-stata

Basic SPSS commands

Although the SPSS commands below are capitalised, they do not have to be capitalised for SPSS to recognise them as commands and run.

LIST: This command will list all the variables in the data set.

DESCRIPTIVES: This command will provide summary statistics for any variable that is mentioned after the command. This would include the mean, standard deviation and range of the variable. You would use this command primarily for continuous variables.

FREQUENCIES: This command provides the frequency distribution of any variable that is mentioned after the command. You would normally use this for categorical variable.

COMPUTE: Use this command to create a new variable.

IF: Use this command to modify the **values** of a variable.

RECODE: Use this command to recode ranges of values of a variable. You can recode the same variable or recode into a new variable.

CROSSTABS: Use this command to construct a two-way table. You would use this command with categorical variables with a few categories. If you have too many categories, the table will be hard to read.

SELECT IF: This selects a subset of the data by reducing the number of cases (individuals) specified in the argument after the command.

SORT CASES: Use this command to sort the data according to a set of variables. You would usually sort the data into ascending or descending values of the Identity variables.

Basic STATA commands

STATA has a number of similar commands to the SPSS commands described above. STATA differentiates between commands written in capitals and lower case, so remember to write the following commands using lower case letters.

summarize: This command is similar to the DESCRIPTIVES command in SPSS and produces the mean, standard deviation and range of the variables that follow the command.

tabulate: If this command is followed by a single variable, this produces a frequency distribution like the FREQUENCIES command in SPSS. If this command is followed by two variables, this produces a two-way table like the CROSSTABS command in SPSS.

generate: This command is similar to the COMPUTE command in SPSS and creates a new variable.

replace . . . if: This command modifies existing variables similar to the IF command in SPSS.

keep if/drop if: This is similar to the SELECT IF command in SPSS and reduces the number of cases in the data. You can also delete variables (columns) in the data using this command.

sort: This is similar to the SORT CASES command in SPSS.

Building a usable data set

Creating subsets of data

The first step to data management is to identify the variable you will be using in your analyses. Some of these variables you will use as is, others you may need to combine or recode. These decisions will depend on the research questions you are trying to answer. It is quite rare that you will use all of the variables included in a data set and quite often data sets are quite large; thus, creating a data set of selected variables is a good idea. These smaller data sets are often easier to manage and require less computing power.

In addition to selecting specific variables, sometimes you may want to create a subset based on specific characteristics of the respondents. For example, if you are interested in comparing job-related stress among younger and older women, you may want a data set which only includes women. You can further subset this data set by restricting the data set to women with children or women in public or private sector occupations. Be careful to not restrict your data too much as you can run into issues of sample size or not having a comparison group.

Wide or long data sets?

Complex data can include repeated questions. This is a feature of longitudinal data; individuals are asked the same questions over time. However, cross-sectional data can also include repeated measures. For example, a study whose focus is on births may ask about all children born to an individual, another study may ask about all of the jobs a person may have had in the past year. Statistical analysis methods may dictate how these data are formatted, that is, the layout of the data.

There are two ways that data may be formatted, wide or long. In a wide-formatted data set, there is one row per individual where each repeated question(s) is in its own column (see Table 5.1).

Table 5.1 Example of a 'wide' data set with one record/person per row

Person	Job 1	Job 2	Job 3	Gender	Age
1	Part-time	Part-time	Full-time	M	40
2	Full-time	Full-time	Full-time	F	25
3	Student			F	22

Note. M = male; F = female.

Analytical methods that require data to be set out in a wide format include **multivariate** analysis of variance (MANOVA), path analyses and growth curve models.

The second way to lay out your data is to have multiple rows for each individual; each row represents one of the repeated questions. This is called a long data set, where repeated measures are stacked on each other. Often with a long data set, some of the responses are repeated, in our example below, gender and age are repeated for each job number. The unit of analysis for a wide data set is the subject, in our example, the person. In Table 5.2, the data in the wide format Table 5.1 have been rearranged into the long format.

Table 5.2 Example of a 'long' data set with multiple rows of data for each person

Person Number	Job Number	Job Description	Gender	Age
1	1	Part-time	M	40
1	2	Part-time	M	40
1	3	Full-time	M	40
2	1	Full-time	F	25
2	2	Full-time	F	25
2	3	Full-time	F	25
3	1	Student	F	22

Note. M = male; F= female.

Analyses which require the use of long-formatted data include panel data analyses, such as fixed effects, mixed models and survival analysis. The unit of analysis for long data sets is usually the measurement occasion within each subject. Nearly all the data sets that are deposited in Data Archives use the wide format, and it is up to the researcher to convert the data to the long format depending on their research question.

Common problems with getting familiar with secondary data sets

Some of the most common problems encountered when you start getting familiar with the data include non-intuitive variable names, no description for **value labels**, changing variable names or value labels between data collection waves, skip patterns and responses to all that apply questions.

Sometimes data sets have variable names which are not intuitive. This may depend on how variable names are created at the time of the questionnaire creation or using an older data set where the data was not originally available for wider use. An example of a non-intuitive variable name would be a variable that indicates whether an individual is male or female being named 'n6501' rather than 'sex'. In these cases, you would need to rename the variable or apply a label that describes the variable. If there are many such variables in the data set, we would suggest you create a data set with the variables you need for your analyses and then rename those few variables rather than spending more time to rename all variables, even those you won't use.

Sometimes the value labels ascribed to a variable will not have a description. This can be quite frustrating as you will need to either ascribe a value or remove that value label. Additionally, if there are missing value codes you may not want to simply set all to missing, but recode specific value codes; however, if you don't know what the value codes mean, you may not be able to do that. An example would be a question that asks about job satisfaction, where the responses range from 1 to 10 but there is no description of the low satisfaction or high satisfaction values. The questionnaires or showcards should provide value labels, which you can then ascribe to the variable. If these are not available, you may need to contact the data provider for clarification.

Longitudinal studies which have been going on for many years or even decades go through many changes. These can include changes in study personnel, content or administrative policy, and all of these can alter how data is presented from wave to wave. As data has become increasingly available for researchers and students to use, the consistency between waves has increased. However, there are still occasions where the same question may have different names or variable labels from one wave of data collection to another. For example, a question about area of residence in England may have undergone many changes throughout the years. For many years, there were eight Standard Statistical Regions, these were then changed to 10 Government Office Regions (GOR) in 1994. There were two additional changes to the GORs in 1998 and 1999, and finally in 2011, GOR became known as regions. All of these may be reflected in one variable over the course of a study. However, the variable name may have changed to reflect the administrative policies; additionally, the description or number of the variable labels may have changed.

Quite often, studies include questions which are only asked of specific groups of people; for example, job stress questions may only be asked of individuals who are currently employed; thus non-employed individuals will not be asked these questions. It is important to understand when this occurs, as it will have implications on your analyses, findings and interpretations of those findings. Often the documentation will provide you with the 'universe' of the sample or the questionnaire will provide skip patterns. Missing value codes may also provide a clue that the question was not asked of everyone. If there is a 'not applicable' missing value code which suddenly becomes larger for certain questions, then it is probable that these were not asked of all individuals.

Often when we make a decision, it is not due to one specific reason, but a combination of reasons. Studies often try to reflect this complex decision-making process by asking individuals to choose all of the answers which may apply to a specific question. However, when preparing the data, sometimes these answers are not adequately labelled or recorded in an intuitive way. Thus, it is important to have a look at the questionnaire for any of these questions and then read the data documentation to understand how data managers included multiple answers to a single question in the data.

As you start on your data management and analysis journey, it is important to remember the following:

1   Data management takes time and is an important step to understanding the data. Do not try to rush through as you will make more mistakes later on by not knowing your data.
2   Search is your friend. Whether this is searching the data documentation or the **raw data**, using a search function will allow you to find what you are looking for faster. This is especially true when working with large complex data sets.
3   You will make mistakes. Even the most seasoned data analyst will make mistakes with data, both new and familiar. Do not get frustrated, try to find where things went wrong and correct the problem.
4   Do not be afraid of asking for help. Whether from other analysts, the institution where the data came from or the internet, help is out there to be had and can make your experience with data much less stressful.

Tips on handling secondary data sets

It is really important to view your data set and get a sense of the numbers that make up your secondary data. You will then get a sense of the scale of the data, how many rows and columns there are and also a visual representation of what the data set looks like in spreadsheet form.

When you open up a data set, have a look at the spreadsheet of numbers underlying the data set. Although these will be mainly columns and rows of numbers, it is really useful to try to read those numbers as a story line. So, for example, if the sampling unit of your data set is individuals, then each row (line) of your data set refers to an individual. You can read information (data) about a specific individual across each of the columns (variables). For survey data sets, typically, each row is a person and each column is a variable.

Often, there will be a lot of columns to read because a data set will hold many variables. The trick is to order your data set so that the important key variables you are interested in are lined up on the left-hand side of your screen. In English, we read text from left to write. While it does not matter for the data set where each of the variables are placed in relation to each other (the columns can be jumbled up), it makes it easier for an English researcher to read a data set if they have the key variables lined up on the left-hand side.

In STATA, this is easy to do, use the *order* command.

In SPSS, you open the data set and *KEEP* the variables in a particular order.

So, for example, order your data set in the following way.

The first column includes your unique identifiers (or key variables). Often there will be just one unique ID variable – if each individual is an independent sample unit. Sometimes you have household members in the same data set, you can have a unique ID for the individual and another unique ID for the household. Let's call the unique ID for the individual person PID and the unique ID for the household (HHID) although these variables are likely to be called something else in different data sets. In which case, when ordering your data set, the first column should be HHID and the second column the PID. Remember to sort the data set so that each row represents all the individuals within the same household (sort HHID PID). You can also do the same clustering if you have geographical variables and you want to see your data set in terms of getting a sense of how many people you have within a particular geographical area.

If your data are longitudinal and in long format, then there will be an indicator of time or data collection period – that is, wave, year, visit, and so on.

The next set of columns are usually demographic data – these are questions that tend to be asked at the start of a survey. So you can order the data set so that gender and age are the next columns.

Go to UKDS, if not already registered, register, create a project and find the ELSA and download the data. Then open the data set wave_1_core_data_v3.

In STATA, the code is

```
use "file location\wave_1_core_data_v3.dta", clear
```

As we are going to be making some changes to the data, we will save a copy of the data and make changes to this copy. This way, if any mistakes are made, we will not overwrite the original data. This is quite important if you are using data from hard to access sources or from sources which have restrictions on the number of times data can be transferred. We use Save to save a copy of the data set that we can then make changes to.

```
save as "file location\wave1_core.dta", clear
```

The next steps would be to identify the key variables and select the variables you will need for your analysis.

When you look at the ELSA data set, you will see that the first four variables are identification variables, two are specific to this data set – that is, *idaindw1* and *idahhw1* – and can be used to identify either households or individuals within the wave. The other two are person specific and can be used to identify people from wave to wave – that is, *idauniq* and *perid*. You may want to choose one, two or all of these; however, be aware of the differences between them and under which circumstances you may use them.

There are some common mistakes that are made when selecting variables from a large data set. These include, but are not limited to, the following:

Selecting the wrong variable for analysis: Sometimes data sets have several variables which seemingly measure the same thing. For example, in the ELSA data set, there are six variables on labour force status; however, in order to use these variables, you will need to rearrange the responses and combine them. Thus, it is important to understand what is in the variable and whether it is the appropriate one to use for your analysis.

Another issue that arises quite often is that some questions are only answered if the respondents answer in a specific way to a previous question – that is, a screener question. For example in ELSA, respondents are only asked if their illness limits their activities if they had answered yes to the previous question about having an illness or disability. However, you may not know this from looking at the data alone; therefore, it is quite important to familiarise yourself with the questionnaire or data documentation as that will often provide information about question routing or the sample to whom the question was asked.

Often individual variables will have missing values. As mentioned earlier in this chapter, reasons for missing are varied, and you may want to recode certain missing codes. Some variables will have negative values, such as income. It is important to make note of these variables and what implications this may have on your analyses. In some cases, you may want to recode the variable so all values are positive; however, this may not always be possible.

Some studies will provide all their data in one data set. However, many studies will provide multiple data sets from which you can select specific variables to merge together into one data set. The ELSA data set that you downloaded contains 58 separate files. Some of these files pertain to an individual wave, there are five files which reference wave 1 and 10 files with a wave 2 reference. It is important to understand what is in each file, often found in the documentation, and to know what variables you need from which files. Finally, it is important to identify the key variable that will allow you to merge the variables together so that you can correctly link each individual's information from several files together. For example, it is possible to merge the financial derived data set to the core data set. We have the option of using one of two identifying variables – that is, *idauniq* and *idaindw1*; however, if we were to merge across waves, say wave 1 to wave 2 data, then we would only use *idauniq*.

Now that you have identified the key variables in the data set, you can sort the data according to those variables, that is, HHID or PID. You may also want to sort by other key variables such as geographic identifier. It is a good idea to keep these key variables together along with some basic demographic data such as age and sex and to place them at the beginning of the data set. This way, when you look at the data, you can easily see composition of the data set according to how you have sorted it.

To sort the ELSA data by personal identification and region, we would do the following:

```
sort idauniq gor
```

Note that this is not the same as sorting by region and then PID, the order of observations in the data set will be different.

```
sort gor idauniq
```

Often data sets have many more variables than you will use in your analyses. The wave 1 core ELSA data set has more than 4000 variables! To reduce confusion, computing power or memory issues and increase manageability, it is advisable to create subsets of the data that are manageable. If you find that you need additional variables, you can always go back to the original data set, get the variable you need and merge it into your smaller data set.

Quite often, you will need to create new variables from ones that are provided in the data set. Earlier in this section, it was noted that some questions are only asked if respondents answer in a specific way to an earlier question. You may want to combine these questions so that you have a variable that includes as many respondents as possible. For example, if you wanted to create a variable that indicates whether an individual in the ELSA data set has a limiting illness or not, then you would do the following:

```
gen limit = helim
replace limit = . if limit == -1
replace limit = 2 if heill == 2
```

This will give you a variable where limit = 1 if they have a limiting illness and 2 if they don't. Note that if you were to tab helim, you will see that there are 5343 with inapplicable and then when you tab limit 5332 are included in the 'no'. Thus, most of the 'inapplicable' were respondents who answered no to heill.

In addition to creating variables, you may also need to recode variables. This will be discussed in depth later; however, remember to create a new variable from the original variable and then recode the newly created variable. This way, if you make a mistake or want to recode in a different way, you can drop the incorrect variable and no changes have been made to the original variable.

Finally, when working on data sets, it is a good idea to create a record of the changes you have made and save the output. The syntax used to create new data sets, variables and analyses can all be saved. In SPSS these are called .sps files, in STATA they are called .do files and in SAS they are called .sas files. Writing your syntax in these files saves time, allows you to reuse or recycle code and share code with co-authors or other researchers. You can also include comments to remind yourself or others what you were doing and why. You can then save your output into files which is useful for later examination or sharing with others. In STATA, output files are .log files, and you would use the following code:

```
log using "file location\filename.log"
```

You can add a ,replace option if you want to overwrite your log file, otherwise you will need to change the filename each time. Some statistical programs such as SAS allow you to export the results to rich text, excel or html files.

Getting to know the Understanding Society data set

Why use the Understanding Society data set?

Understanding Society is a rich and valuable data resource that provides high-quality, longitudinal information on topics such as education, employment, health, income, family and ethnicity. Understanding Society data helps researchers understand the short-, middle- and long-term effects of social and economic change.

If you are new to using longitudinal data, the CLOSER Learning Hub (https://learning.closer.ac.uk) has information and resources to help you explore longitudinal studies.

Contents of the study

Understanding Society is longitudinal, and the data have been collected over a long term. By repeatedly collecting data from the same individuals over many years, changes in people's lives can be understood and causality can be better identified than with cross-sectional survey data. Data collection for the BHPS, which is now part of Understanding Society, started in 1991, whilst Understanding Society data collection started in 2009–2010.

The Study has a household focus. The collection of data from every adult and child aged 10 years or older in each household means that inter-relations between family and household members can be investigated. The large sample size permits analysis of small subgroups and analysis at regional and country levels.

Target population and samples

Understanding Society has four core samples:

1   A sample of around 26,000 households, representative for the residential population living in private households in the UK in 2009–2010
2   An Ethnic Minority Boost sample for England and Wales designed to provide around 1000 adult respondents from Indian, Pakistani, Bangladeshi, Caribbean and African groups
3   An Immigrant and Ethnic Minority Boost sample added at wave 6 to add a sample of new immigrants and refresh the core ethnic minority groups
4   Households from the BHPS, which was a representative probability sample of the residential population living in private households in Britain in 1991, with subsequent boost samples for Scotland, Wales and Northern Ireland. You can find out more about the BHPS at https://www.iser.essex.ac.uk/bhps

In the data, information from all samples in a single wave is presented in the same files. When analysing data from Understanding Society, it is important to consider that not all cases had the same probability of selection into the study originally and that all samples (except the Northern Ireland sample) used a clustered and stratified design. The study attempts to maintain individuals from the first wave as part of the sample as long as they live in the UK. The study also interviews other individuals joining their household, as long as they live with the original sample member.

Accessing the data

You can access the data through the UKDS, and users are required to register with the UKDS to access the data.

Using the data

The data are delivered in a file containing a compressed folder named UKDA-6641-stata, which you need to extract using software such as 7-Zip. The data are available in STATA, SPSS or TAB formats. When you open the compressed folder and click on Extract in the task bar, the Extraction Wizard starts. You are prompted to choose a location to place the extracted files. We recommend you keep all files in a designated folder, and as our data gets updated over time it is advisable to include the release version in the folder name.

Once you have extracted the file, you will find two files and two folders. The file read6614.htm links to a website that provides basic information about this release. The file 6614_file_information provides a list of all files in this release. Detailed study documentation, such as user guides, questionnaires and fieldwork materials are in the subfolder mrdoc/pdf.

The Understanding Society data are in the subfolder stata\stata11_se. This contains the data files in wave-specific subfolders. For example, bhps_w1 contains all data files from harmonised BHPS files from its first wave, us_w1 contains all data files from Understanding Society wave 1. The respective cross-wave files are in bhps_wx and us_wx.

Data structure

Data files

Data for different waves are presented in separate files. File names begin with a prefix designating the wave of data collection ("a_" for the first wave, "b_" for the second wave; we use "w_" to denote waves in general). Waves collected before 2009 additionally have a "b" in front of the wave prefix (i.e. "bw_"). A small number of files do not have wave prefixes – they store information across all waves.

Data collected from different sources (e.g. the household interview, the adult interview and the youth interview) are stored in separate files. Table 5.3 lists the key data files that contain substantive information collected in interviews with responding households and individuals. The root filename is fixed over time.

Table 5.3 Key data files for analysing data for responding households and individuals in Understanding Society and the British Household Panel Study

Filename	Description
bw_hhresp	Substantive data from responding BHPS households
w_hhresp	Substantive data from responding UKHLS households
bw_indresp	Substantive data for responding adults (16+ years), including proxies and telephone
w_indresp	interviews from individual questionnaires, including self-completion
bw_youth	Substantive data from the youth questionnaire (UKHLS: age 10–15 years, all waves)
w_youth	Harmonised BHPS: age 11–15 years, waves 4–18 only
xwavedat	Includes stable characteristics of individuals, including those reported when first entering the study

Note. BHPS = British Household Panel Study; UKHLS = UK Household Longitudinal Study.

Identifiers

When you open a file, it will contain variables that identify the units of observation such as households and individuals.

Households are identified by *w_hidp*, a wave (w)-specific variable with a different prefix for each wave. It can be used to link information about a household from different records within a wave but cannot be used to link information across waves.

Individuals are identified by the personal identifier (*pidp*), which is consistent in all waves and can be used to link information about a person from different records belonging to one wave or to link information from different waves. Additionally, individuals are identified by *w_pno* – the person number within the household in a single wave. The combination of *w_hidp* and *w_pno* is unique for each individual.

Variable names and conventions

Variable names are built from the wave prefix and the variable root name. The variable root name does not change over time as long as the underlying question does not change substantially. The prefix designates the wave of data collection (i.e. bw_ for waves collected before 2009 or w_ for waves collected from 2009 onwards) and is not used for information that will, by definition, never change (e.g. the unique cross-wave person identifier *pidp* and the survey design variables *psu* and strata) or stable characteristics in the data file *xwavedat*.

The variable root name corresponds to the name used for questions in the questionnaire, so it is easy to look up the questions that underpin the data. The Universe field in the questionnaire provides users with information about who gets asked a specific question.

Information about variables can be found in the online data set documentation. You can use the Index of Terms to search for variables most suitable for your research.

For various reasons, survey responses may not have a valid code or value. Table 5.4 lists the types of missing information that we differentiate between in our data. All missing values are negative and are never used as valid responses.

Table 5.4 Missing value codes in Understanding Society and the British Household Panel Study

Value	Description
−21	No data from the UKHLS
−20	No data from BHPS waves 1–18
−11	Only available for the IEMBS
−10	Not available for the IEMBS
−9	Missing by error or implausible
−8	Not applicable to the person or because of routing
−7	Proxy respondent. The question was not asked of proxy respondent or derived variable cannot be computed for proxy respondents
−2	Respondent refused
−1	Respondent does not know the answer

Note. BHPS = British Household Panel Study; IEMBS = Immigrant and Ethnic Minority Boost Study; UKHLS = UK Household Longitudinal Study.

The variable view is the best place to find out more about variables that are produced post-field. In the data, additional variables are positioned at the bottom of the data files. It is a good idea to look at the variables already derived by the Understanding Society team (search for *_dv in your STATA file). These are variables that have been through some quality checking by the Understanding Society team, and so that increases your confidence that they can be used for research purposes. Moreover, these derived variables are often created for commonly used variables – for example, the highest level of educational qualifications obtained. This is made up of lots of questions about qualifications.

Key variables

A table of Understanding Society key variables for the analysis of individual response data can be found here.

If you are interested in the individual responses of Understanding Society participants, the key variables shown in Table 5.5 are included in the indresp data files in all waves. Variables that are only available in waves prior to 2009 are marked with the prefix bw_.

Table 5.5 Key variables in the Understanding Society data sets

Topic Domain	Variable Name	Short Description
Identifiers	pidp	Unique cross-wave person identifier
	w_hidp	Within-wave household identifier
	w_pno	Person within-wave household id
Locality	w_country	Country in the UK
	w_gor_dv	Region in the UK
	w_urban_dv	Urban or rural area, derived
Demographic characteristics	w_age_dv	Age at time of interview, derived
	ukborn	Born in UK
	w_sex_dv	Sex, derived
	w_marstat	Marital status
	w_jbstat	Employment status
	racel_dv	Ethnicity
	w_nchild_dv	Number of children in the household. Includes natural children, adopted children and stepchildren, under the age of 16 years
Socio-economic characteristics	w_hiqual_dv	Highest qualification
	w_jbsoc00_cc	Standard Socio-economic Classification (SOC 2000) of current job. Condensed three-digit version
	w_jbnssec8_dv	Current job: Eight Class NS-SEC
	w_jbnssec5_dv	Current job: Five Class NS-SEC
	w_jbnssec3_dv	Current job: Three Class NS-SEC
	w_fimnnet_dv	Own total estimated net monthly income
	w_fimnlabnet_dv	Own total estimated net monthly income from labour
Health	w_sf12mcs_dv	SF-12: mental health component score, derived
	w_sf12pcs_dv	SF-12: physical health component score, derived
	w_health	Long-standing illness or disability
	w_scghq1_dv	Subjective well-being (GHQ): Likert-type
	w_scghq2_dv	Subjective well-being (GHQ): Caseness
Individual and family background	scend_dv	School-leaving age
	j1soc00_cc	Standard Socio-economic Classification (SOC 2000) of first job after leaving full-time education. Condensed three-digit version
	maid	Mother's ethnic group

Topic Domain	Variable Name	Short Description
	macob	Mother's country of birth
	maedqf	Mother's educational qualification when respondent was aged 14 years
	masoc90_cc masoc00_cc masoc10_cc	Standard Occupational Classification 1990/2000/2010 of mother's job when respondent was aged 14 years
	paid	Father's ethnic group
	pacob	Father's country of birth
	paedqf	Father's educational qualification when respondent was aged 14 years
	pasoc90_cc pasoc00_cc pasoc10_cc	Standard Occupational Classification 1990/2000/2010 of father's job when respondent was aged 14 years
Household-level characteristics	w_hhsize	Number of individuals in the household
	w_nkids_dv	Number of children aged under 16 years in the household
	w_hhtype_dv	Household composition
	w_tenure_dv	Housing tenure
	w_fihhmnnet1_dv	Net household monthly income
	w_ieqmoecd_dv	Household income conversion factor (modified OECD scale)

Note. NS-SEC = National Statistics Socio-economic Classification; SF-12 = Short Form–12; GHQ = General Health Questionnaire; OECD = Organisation for Economic Co-operation and Development.

Variables without a wave prefix can be merged in from the *xwavedat* data file using *pidp*.

Household-level characteristics variables are from the household data file (*hhresp*) and can be merged in using *w_hidp*.

Practical exercise

Open up the Understanding Society data set.

Keep just the variables you are interested in.

How many variables are left in your data set?

Did you keep the ID variables?

Understanding Society common STATA commands

To load the whole data file:

```
use a_indresp, clear
```

To load specific variables of file:

> use pidp a_hidp a_pno a_sex_dv a_hiqual_dv a_nchild_dv using a_indresp, clear

Commonly used commands to explore data

To check if pidp uniquely identifies each row of the data file and produces an error if this is not the case:

> isid pidp

To show the frequency distribution of the number of rows with the same value of each household identifier variable:

> duplicates report a_hidp

To display variable type, format and any value and variable labels attached to the variable:

> describe a_hiqual_dv

To count the number of rows or observations for whom a_hiqual_dv is missing:

> count if a_hiqual_dv<0

Count can be used with more complicated logical statements. For example, count the number of women with degree or higher qualifications.

> count if a_hiqual_dv==1 & a_sex_dv==2

To show a histogram of the variable specified, number of missing or zero observations:

> inspect a_nchild_dv

To show the overview of variable type, stats, number of missing unique values:

> codebook a_hiqual_dv a_nchild_dv

To print out a few cases on STATA screen use list, use the list command. This example below will list out the a_hidp a_pno a_hiqual_dv for observations with a_nchild_dv ==2 and separate out the list by each household identifier.

> list a_hidp a_pno a_hiqual_dv if a_nchild_dv ==2, sepby(a_hidp)

This example below will list out the a_hidp a_pno a_hiqual_dv for first 10 observations.

list a_hidp a_pno a_hiqual_dv in 1/10

To open the data editor and allow you to browse the data file:

browse

Commonly used commands to modify and sort the data file

To recode missing values (which are given SPECIFIC NEGATIVE VALUES –9 –8 –7 –2 –1) to missing values that STATA can recognise as missing value [.]:

recode a_hiqual_dv (–9/–1=.)

OR

replace a_hiqual_dv=. if a_hiqual_dv==–9 | a_hiqual_dv==–8 | a_hiqual_dv==–7| a_hiqual_dv==–2 | a_hiqual_dv==–1

OR

mvdecode a_hiqual_dv, mv(–9/–1)

To sort in order of the variables specified, that is, first by a_hidp and then within each a_hidp value by value of a_pno (the default is to sort in ascending order):

gsort a_hidp a_pno

Commonly used commands to summarise data

To display summary statistics (mean, stdev, min, max) for the variables specified:

summarize a_hiqual_dv a_nchild_dv

To display a one-way table – number of rows with each value of a_hiqual_dv:

tabulate a_hiqual_dv

To display a one-way table – number of rows with each value of a_hiqual_dv, including the missing values (.):

tabulate a_hiqual_dv, missing

To display a one-way table and create a series of (0–1) binary variables for every a_hiqual_dv value with names hiqual1, hiqual2, . . .:

tabulate a_hiqual_dv, missing gen(hiqual)

To display a two-way table – cross tabulate number of observations for each combination of a_hiqual_dv and a_nchild_dv:

tabulate a_hiqual_dv a_nchild_dv, missing

To display a compact table of summary statistics:

tabstat a_nchild_dv, by(a_hiqual_dv) stat(mean sd n)

To display a flexible table of summary statistics, display stats formats numbers for all data:

table a_hiqual_dv, contents(mean a_nchild_dv sd a_nchild_dv) f(%9.2fc) row

Chapter Summary

- Data from data archives will often come in various formats for use in different statistical software packages such as SPSS, STATA or SAS.
- There should be an option for getting the data in text format, which can be read by all software packages.
- Although both SPSS and STATA have windows point and click buttons, it is highly advisable for any secondary data researcher to become familiar with some of the basic commands in these statistical packages.
- The first step to data management is to identify the variables you will be using in your analyses. Some of these variables you will use as is, others you may need to combine or recode. These decisions will depend on the research questions you are trying to answer.
- Some of the most common problems encountered when you start getting familiar with the data include non-intuitive variable names, no description for value labels, changing variable names or value labels between data collection waves, skip patterns and responses to all that apply questions.
- As you start on your data management and analysis journey, it is important to remember the following:

  1 Data management takes time and is an important step to understanding the data.
  2 Searching through published documentation is crucial.
  3 You will make mistakes so keep a record of everything you do with the data.
  4 Do not be afraid of asking for help, especially through online resources.

- To reduce confusion, computing power or memory issues and increase manageability, it is advisable to create subsets of the data that are manageable.
- Finally, when working on data sets, it is a good idea to create a record of the changes you have made and save the output.

Further Reading

Longhi, S., & Nandi, A. (2020). *A practical guide to using panel data*. Sage.

6

MANIPULATING DATA AND BASIC STATISTICAL ANALYSIS

TARANI CHANDOLA AND CARA BOOKER

Chapter Overview

Background 70

Examining univariate distributions 70

Examining bivariate associations 77

Examining multivariate associations 87

Basic longitudinal data analysis 93

Practical longitudinal data analysis exercise 95

Further Reading 105

Background

There is some overlap of the contents of this chapter with the books in this *SAGE Quantitative Research Kit* series. However, this chapter will concentrate more on the 'how to' aspect of statistical analysis, rather than the underlying theory. We also have some suggestions on basic data manipulations in SPSS and STATA. Often the data you get from the data archives are not immediately suitable for statistical analysis. These **variables** may be in the 'raw' form – direct answers to questions. A lot of the times, this raw data needs to be transformed into something more meaningful for analysis. An example of this is when you have a question with lots of possible responses (say more than 20 responses). Trying to analyse a variable with more than 20 categories is not easy, so you need to find a way to reduce the complexity of 20 categories into something easier to analyse. The trouble is in doing so, you could lose some of the complexity of the data, but in return, you might be able to see patterns with fewer categories that were not immediately evident with all the 20 categories.

This chapter will show you how to select the variables you want, explore their value codes and distributions and transform raw variables into analysis-ready variables. Our first example will focus on cross-sectional data and analysis, while the second example will focus on longitudinal analysis.

For both of these examples, we will use the UKHLS data set. Our research questions are as follows:

> *Example 1:* Who has more job stress – those with the highest or the lowest educational qualifications?
>
> *Example 2:* Does well-being change when one becomes unemployed?

Examining univariate distributions

When you are looking at the distribution of a particular variable in a data set, make sure you read the original question and try to answer the question yourself. What response would you have chosen? What do you think should be the expected distribution of this variable? If it is a question about how stressed people feel about their job, do you think most people would report that they felt tense about their job most of the time? To have a sense of the expected distribution, you need to read from the literature how this question (or a related question) is distributed in other surveys.

Most of the time, with **Likert scales**, the modal response is somewhere in the middle, and rarely at the extremes of the responses. In most cultures, there is a strong psychological preference not to go for the extremes. Also, the fact that your data set comes from a general population sample rather than a sample of people who are clinically depressed will also affect your expected distributions of stress. If you had asked this question in a highly stressed out group – for example, patients attending a clinic on stress – you might expect a different distribution with most people saying they felt tense most of the time.

Have a look at the expected distributions of the variable from the data set. Make sure that you replicate this distribution from other findings from published reports and papers. It is really important to do this to make sure you understand the data. Make sure you take into account realistic **values** of the variable. The convention is to have negative values for some categorical variables, and these tend to represent different types of missing data.

Example

Job stress questions are first asked in wave 2, so we will be using this wave for this example. All UKHLS data sets have a letter prefix that corresponds with the wave – that is, wave 1 = a_, wave 2 = b_, and so on.

Step 1: select variables you will be using in analysis.

We will be using the b_indresp datafile. This datafile has 1615 variables, which are quite a lot, and you will not need to use all of them. We will then select the specific variables we want to use.

For this example, we will use the following variables:

Job stress:	b_depenth1 to b_depenth6
Educational qualification:	b_hiqual_dv
Age:	b_dvage
Gender:	b_sex
Key variables:	pidp, b_hidp

The type of variable and their value codes can be found in the UKHLS online data documentation. Figure 6.1 is an example of what you will see when you look up the variables.

The UKHLS data documentation tells us that only people in paid work answers this question (as only people who 'did paid work last week or did no paid work last week but have a job' were asked this question). This is why there are 22,343 persons who are inapplicable to answer this question as they did not have a paid job. The exact wording of the question is also provided. At the end of the page, you can see that these questions are only asked every 2 years, on the even years. This variable, b_depenth1, and the other variables that can be summed to create a scale, b_depenth1 to b_depenth6, are ranked **categorical variables** (or **ordinal variables**), part of a Likert scale.

Datafile: b_indresp

Related to 1 Questions

workconditions_w2.depenth1
Feels tense about job

Universe	if CURRENTEMPLOYMENT.JBHAS = 1	CURRENTEMPLOYMENT.JBOFF = 1 (did paid work last week or did no paid work last week but has a job)
Text	Thinking of the past few weeks, how much of the time has your job made you feel tense?

Associated variables

- b_depenth1 (b_indresp) feels tense about job

Frequencies

Value label	Value	Absolute frequency	Relative frequency	
missing	-9	3	0.01%	
inapplicable	-8	22343	40.95%	▉
proxy	-7	3880	7.11%	▉
refusal	-2	2	0.0%	
don't know	-1	77	0.14%	
never	1	6492	11.9%	▉
occasionally	2	9695	17.77%	▉
some of the time	3	8026	14.71%	▉
most of the time	4	3180	5.83%	▉
all of the time	5	866	1.59%		
	Total	54564	100.0%	

Index Term

- Employment: Attitude to Work and Incentives

Wave Occurrences
2, 4, 6, 8

Figure 6.1 Distribution of b_depenth 'feels tense about job' from wave 2 of Understanding Society

From the data documentation, we can see all negative values are different missing codes. As these questions were only asked of a specific subgroup, the -8 (inapplicable) values are not 'missing' but indicate the numbers who were not asked this question, or series of questions. The code of -9 is for genuine missing responses. This variable had very few (only three) people. This indicates that the vast majority of people did not find it problematic to answer this question. Very often, if a question is problematic, there will be lots of missing values. So a question can be a sensitive question, like a person's sexuality or their income. Typically, these questions have a lot of missing data. Or else, a question can be hard to understand, so people will skip responding to the question and move on to the next question. There were also a number of people for whom others – that is, a proxy – answered selected questions for them; however, these questions or set of questions were not asked of proxy respondents. Finally, we have a small number of respondents who either did not know the answer ($n = 77$) to this question or refused to provide an answer ($n = 2$).

While the distributions are given here, we will calculate them again as part of our data management steps. Take note that these are not weighted distributions.

A proxy interview is an interview with someone (e.g. parent, spouse) other than the person about whom information is being sought. Proxy interviews with another household member, or telephone interviews, are carried out for eligible members who are either too ill or too busy to be interviewed. A proxy schedule is used to collect information about household members absent throughout the field period or too old or infirm to complete the interview themselves. It is administered to another member of the household, with preference shown for the spouse or adult child. The questionnaire is a much shortened version of the individual questionnaire, collecting some demographic, health and employment details, as well as a summary income measure.

Typically, subjective questions about attitudes are not asked of proxies, as only the person can meaningfully report about their own feelings. So this question about how the job makes them feel cannot be answered by a proxy person. Hence, the code for a proxy respondent for subjective questions is very useful.

From Figure 6.2, we can see that this variable is a derived variable that originates from the b_indall datafile. Because age is a continuous variable, we are provided descriptive statistics different from those provided for categorical variables – that is, means and standard deviations compared to absolute and relative frequencies. This variable is computed at every wave. Since age is an important variable and relatively easy to calculate due to having both date of birth and date of interview, this variable is less likely to have missing data. Thus, as you can see, the total sample size 54,564 is the same as the total absolute frequency for b_depenth1. However, b_depenth1 will have fewer valid responses due to missing data.

To select only these variables from the larger data set, we can use the following STATA commands:

```
use "file location \b_indresp", clear

keep pidp b_hidp b_dvage b_sex b_depenth1 b_depenth2 b_depenth3 b_depenth4
b_depenth5 b_depenth6 b_hiqual_dv
```

b_dvage
age (computed)

Datafile: b_indresp

Related to 1 Questions

hhgrid_w2.dvage
Age (computed)

Associated variables
- b_dvage (b_indresp) age (computed)
- b_dvage (b_indall) age (computed)

Derived Variable Note

The age of the respondent at last birthday. This is derived from the exact date of birth and the date of the interview. Where the date of birth information is missing, the estimated age is used. Note the change in definition in Wave 6.

See B_AGE_DV

Origin

Uses B_DVAGE on data file B_INDALL

Statistics

Mean	Number Missing	Min	Max	Std Dev	N
46.63	0	16.0	102.0	18.46	54564

Index Terms
- Derived Variables
- Socio-demographic Characteristics

Wave Occurrences
1, 2, 3, 4, 5, 6, 7, 8

Figure 6.2 Distribution of b_dvage 'age' from wave 2 of Understanding Society

The above commands result in a much smaller data set of wave 2 individuals from Understanding Society with just the individual and household identifiers (pipd and b_hidp), age (b_dvage), sex (b_sex), the job stress questions (b_depenth1 to b_depenth6) and highest educational qualifications (b_hiqual_dv). We have a mix of categorical and continuous variables in our data set, which requires different commands to explore the distributions. We will use frequencies to explore the categorical variables and means to explore the continuous ones. The STATA **fre** command is useful for examining univariate distributions of variables (and is similar to the **FREQUENCY** command in SPSS). However, it is not part of the standard set of STATA commands. So you will need to first run and install this particular command, before using the command.

ssc install fre

fre b_sex

Table 6.1 shows the distribution of sex at wave 2 of Understanding Society. We can observe that there are more women than men in the data set. Note that the numbers in these tables (*n* = 54,569) are slightly larger than those from the data documentation (*n* = 54,564). This is due to using an updated version of the data for the analysis compared to the data used to create the data documentation.

Table 6.1 Distribution of b_sex 'sex' at wave 2 of Understanding Society

b_sex — sex

		Freq.	Percent	Valid	Cum.
Valid	1 male	25044	45.87	45.87	45.87
	2 female	29553	54.13	54.13	100.00
	Total	54597	100.00	100.00	

fre b_depenth1

Table 6.2 shows that very few people feel tense about their job most or all of the time.

Table 6.2 Distribution of b_depenth1 'feels tense about job' at wave 2 of Understanding Society

b_depenth1 — feels tense about job

		Freq.	Percent	Valid	Cum.
Valid	-9 missing	3	0.01	0.01	0.01
	-8 inapplicable	22360	40.95	40.95	40.96
	-7 proxy	3882	7.11	7.11	48.07
	-2 refused	2	0.00	0.00	48.07
	-1 don't know	77	0.14	0.14	48.22
	1 never	6496	11.90	11.90	60.11
	2 occasionally	9699	17.76	17.76	77.88
	3 some of the time	8030	14.71	14.71	92.59
	4 most of the time	3182	5.83	5.83	98.41
	5 all of the time	866	1.59	1.59	100.00
	Total	54597	100.00	100.00	

```
fre b_hiqual_dv
```

Note that in Table 6.3, there were very few people with missing data for this variable, so this makes it a very useful variable for analysis. It can be quite complex to create this variable, as it depends on responses to many questions about a person's educational history. The availability of a derived variable that summarises this complexity and is more or less completely available for everyone in the sample, makes this an ideal variable to use in research (so long as it is relevant to your research question).

Table 6.3 Distribution of b_hiqual_dv 'highest qualification' at wave 2 of Understanding Society

```
b_hiqual_dv — Highest qualification, UKHLS & BHPS samples
```

		Freq.	Percent	Valid	Cum.
Valid	-9 Missing	69	0.13	0.13	0.13
	-8 Inapplicable	566	1.04	1.04	1.16
	1 Degree	11372	20.83	20.83	21.99
	2 Other higher degree	5940	10.88	10.88	32.87
	3 A-level etc	11115	20.36	20.36	53.23
	4 GCSE etc	11469	21.01	21.01	74.24
	5 Other qualification	5438	9.96	9.96	84.20
	9 No qualification	8628	15.80	15.80	100.00
	Total	54597	100.00	100.00	

```
sum b_dvage
```

As age is a continuous variable, we would normally not use the 'fre' command, but instead use another command like 'summ' to summarise the distribution of age (see Table 6.4; the STATA command **summ** is similar to the SPSS command **DESCRIPTIVES**). Just like sex, there should be no missing data for age. If your data set has a lot of missing data for basic demographic variables like age and sex, then it is possible that the data could be of poor quality, or else you might have accidentally done something to the data set and inadvertently created a number of cases with missing age or sex data. Checking the distributions of variables like age and sex is an easy way of checking your data set, especially if you have made complex changes to the data set.

Table 6.4 Distribution of b_dvage 'age' at wave 2 of Understanding Society

Variable	Obs	Mean	Std. Dev.	Min	Max
b_dvage	54,597	46.63423	18.45751	16	102

The STATA commands highlighted above can also be replicated in SAS. Here is an example of a SAS code to examine the univariate distribution of the variables.

SAS code:

For categorical variables:

```
proc freq data=b_indresp;
tables b_sex b_depenth1 b_depenth2 b_depenth3 b_depenth4 b_depenth5
b_depenth6;
run;
```

For continuous variables:

```
proc means data=b_indresp;
var b_sex;
run;
```

Examining bivariate associations

Manipulating data

Manipulation is often used in a negative context, but it does not always have to be negative, for example, clothing designers manipulate fabric or origami is the manipulation of paper. The key is to not over-manipulate or torture the data in order to get the results you want. You should make sure to have very clear research questions, hypotheses and data strategies prior to starting your data analyses.

One relatively minor way to manipulate the data is to recode the missing values for the variables of interest.

Here, we will set all missing values codes to missing so that the statistical program will ignore them from now on. Alternatives would be to set the -8 or inapplicable to zero in order to keep sample members not in paid work in the analyses.

```
recode b_depenth1-b_depenth6 (-9/-1=.)
recode b_hiqual_dv (-9/-8)=.
```

Another way of manipulating data is to combine response categories. There are two ways to determine whether this is an appropriate action. One is based on the distribution of the categories and the other is based on theory. Often researchers use a mixture of both to determine whether they should reduce category numbers.

The derived variable for educational qualifications is a six-category variable. We will discuss whether we should collapse some of these categories together.

The smallest category is the 'other qualification'. What does it mean? Usually, this is for people with non-UK qualifications which they cannot translate into A- or O-level qualifications. Some people merge this with the no qualifications group, but that would mean losing valuable information, such as the fact that they received their education outside the UK. But on the other hand, if someone has got qualifications that are not easily translated into the UK context, then they may find it just as hard to find a job as someone with no qualifications. The type of work they find may be very similar to someone who is UK born but with no qualifications. So there are arguments on both sides as to whether or not to merge these two groups together. Often people use one justification over another. That is OK, so long as you make it explicit what you have chosen and detail the reasons you have chosen. This makes it easy for other people to check what you have done and check your assumptions.

Always generate new variables when you recode. Try not to recode and overwrite the original variable. This is because often you may change your mind about the recode (or some other transformation you did), and you may wish to recode things another way (or do some other transformation). However, it is often very hard to get back to the original variable if you have overwritten it during the recode. So it is just good practice to keep your original variable, but generate a new one that is the same as the original variable which you then manipulate (recode). If you don't think that the manipulated variable is the correct one, just discard it (drop . . .) and go back to the original one and start again.

When generating new variables, there are a few simple things to remember:

1   Use meaningful variable names.
2   Use value and variable labels.
3   When generating binary variables (0/1), use 1 to indicate the event or concept you are interested in.

So if we wanted to create a new educational qualifications variable with only five categories where we combine the 'other qualifications' category with the 'no qualifications' category, we would use the following code.

*Generating new variable for educational qualifications

```
gen b_hiqual_dv5 = b_hiqual_dv
```

*Recode b_hiqual_dv5: no qualification (9) to same category as other qualification (5), this allows the user to keep the variable coded as 1-5 rather than 1-4,9

```
recode b_hiqual_dv5 9=5
```

Cross tabulations

When creating cross tabulations, it may be easier to recode your key variables into binary variables. This is because 2 × 2 tables are easier to read and understand than larger tables. For example, we can recode the five categories in each of the b_depenth variables into just two categories. However, we need to decide what our cut-off points will be. Should it be at 2 (occasionally), 3 (some of the time) or 4 (most of the time). The following are some recommendations:

1. What makes sense theoretically? Does 'never and occasionally' go more together than 'never, occasionally and some of the time'? Is the response 'some of the time' an indicator of work stress in such a way that it fits in more with 4 = most of the time and 5 = all of the time more so than with 1 = never and 2 = occasionally?

2. What is the distribution? For binary variables, you need to have enough people in each category. How much is enough? Usually, we need at least five people in each cell of a table. Now UKHLS is a very big study, so that usually is not a problem. There are usually enough people who choose the extremes, given the size of the survey. However, it still makes sense to look at the percentage distribution of each category. You will see that fewer than 10% choose most of the time and all of the time. In a smaller data set with just a few hundred people sampled, having such a small category could be problematic for constructing 2 × 2 tables and making statistical inference. So it may make more sense to combine group 3 with groups 4 and 5 in order to have enough people who say that their work makes them tense.

3. See what other people have done. This is probably the weakest argument to make, as other people may not have been correct in their methods. Also, if it is a new variable, there may not be any information from other studies.

To Construct the 2 × 2 Table

Just like we have conventions for figures, where we place independent variables on the x (horizontal) axis and dependent variables on the y (vertical) axis, it is useful to keep that similar pattern for tables. Try to place your dependent variables as the columns (vertical axis) and your independent variables as the rows (horizontal axis). Then you need to choose between row and column percentages.

Here, we look at the cross tabulation of gender and a recoded b_depenth1 variable and examine the row percentages.

*Recoding b_depenth1 into b_depenth1_b in STATA

```
gen b_depenth1_b = b_depenth1
recode b_depenth1_b 1=0 2/5=1
```

*Creating cross tabulation in STATA

```
tab2 b_depenth1_b b_sex, row
```

Table 6.5 displays the row percentages, so we should be comparing the figures in the rows. The table tells us that among those who feel tense about their jobs, there are more women (53%) than men (47%).

If you wanted column percentages, then do the following:

tab2 b_depenth1_b b_sex, col nofreq

Table 6.5 Cross tabulation of sex and b_depenth1 'feels tense about job' at wave 2 of Understanding Society: row percentages

b_depenth1 _b	sex		
	male	female	Total
0	50.66	49.34	100.00
1	46.82	53.18	100.00
Total	47.70	52.30	100.00

Table 6.6 shows a larger percentage of females feel tense about their jobs compared to males. Remember to compare the percentages in the columns when you choose column percentages. One of the most common mistakes in presenting tables is choosing the wrong type of percentage to display. If we follow the rule that the 'dependent' variable is placed on the *y*-axis (the column) and the 'independent' variable is placed on the *x*-axis (the row), then usually it makes sense to choose column percentages. This is because we are interested in seeing how the dependent variable (units of *y*) changes as the independent variable (units of *x*, which are the rows) changes. We are interested in comparing people in the columns, but we need to have equal proportions of people in the columns to compare the figures in the columns. The column percentages add up to 100%, so this makes it easy to compare the figures in the columns.

Table 6.6 Cross tabulation of sex and b_depenth1 'feels tense about job' at wave 2 of Understanding Society: column percentages

b_depenth1 _b	sex		
	male	female	Total
0	24.40	21.68	22.98
1	75.60	78.32	77.02
Total	100.00	100.00	100.00

Correlations

Correlations are usually for interval variables (with a continuous distribution), although sometimes people use correlations to measure associations between ordinal variables. Therefore, we will be using the original variables rather than the newly generated ones.

We would like to examine whether educational qualifications is really a linear variable. The job stress variables are already in a Likert scale, so we will treat them as ordinal variables:

    pwcorr b_depenth1 hiqual_dv, sig

The Pearson correlation is –0.0792.

This correlation signifies that a higher score on the educational qualification variables (fewer qualifications) is associated with lower score on the b_depenth1 variables – that is, towards the never end of the scale rather than at the always end of the scale. Sometimes negative correlations can be difficult to interpret, so it may be useful to reverse code your variables. In this case, if we were to recode educational qualifications so that higher scores mean more qualifications, we would get the same number, but it would be positive. It is also arguably more easy to interpret, with those with higher qualifications being more likely to report that they are tense about their job all the time.

Also note that the correlation is significant but weak. It is significant just because of the sheer size of the UKHLS, so significance is not so useful for correlation coefficients when we have large sample sizes. Instead, we need to look at the effect size, and here the interpretation is that a 1 standard deviation (SD) increase in qualification is associated with a 0.08 SD increase in work tension.

How meaningful is this?

We may also want to look at correlations between variables that may make up a scale, that is, depenth1 to depenth6:

    pwcorr b_depenth1 b_depenth2 b_depenth3 b_depenth4 b_depenth5 b_depenth6, sig

In Table 6.7, the correlations range from 0.48 to 0.76, these equate to moderate to high correlations.

Table 6.7 Correlation of the job stress variables from wave 2 of Understanding Society

	b_depe~1	b_depe~2	b_depe~3	b_depe~4	b_depe~5	b_depe~6
b_depenth1	1.0000					
b_depenth2	0.6473 0.0000	1.0000				
b_depenth3	0.5898 0.0000	0.6684 0.0000	1.0000			
b_depenth4	0.4814 0.0000	0.5294 0.0000	0.5358 0.0000	1.0000		
b_depenth5	0.5047 0.0000	0.5418 0.0000	0.5292 0.0000	0.7194 0.0000	1.0000	
b_depenth6	0.5006 0.0000	0.5337 0.0000	0.5062 0.0000	0.7090 0.0000	0.7613 0.0000	1.0000

This indicates that the variables may be tapping in to the same underlying construct. You can also see variables b_depenth4 to b_depenth6 have much stronger correlations (more than 0.70) compared to the correlations with the other variables. Looking through the exact questions, you see that they correspond to much more negatively worded emotions such as gloomy, miserable and depressed. So someone saying that they are feeling gloomy most of the time are also much more likely to report feeling miserable or depressed most of the time, much more so than someone saying that they feel tense, worried or uneasy.

If we want to see the internal consistency or get an idea of whether these variables may measure the same basic concept, we would use an alpha test:

alpha b_depenth1 b_depenth2 b_depenth3 b_depenth4 b_depenth5 b_depenth6

The reliability coefficient from this command is 0.8917 which is well above the recommended 0.70. So it may be useful to combine these six variables into a single variable. In this case, our variables have good internal consistency, and we can combine them; however, in other cases you may want to use other methods to see if there are subscales or whether some variables go better together than others. Methods for determining this include factor analysis and principal component analysis (PCA).

To generate our mean score of job stress variables, we have two options, the difference between these are how the coding treats missing variables.

gen b_depenthsum=(b_depenth1 +b_depenth2+ b_depenth3 +b_depenth4+ b_depenth5+ b_depenth6)/6

versus

egen b_depenthmean=rowmean(b_depenth1 b_depenth2 b_depenth3 b_depenth4 b_depenth5 b_depenth6)

The former will result in 28,238 observations, whereas the latter will result in 41 more observations, 28,279. This is because the former is only calculated on complete cases – people who have responded to every single question on work stress. However, the latter is calculated taking the mean of whatever responses are available. If someone has answered only five questions, then the mean of those five questions is calculated (rather than dropping this case or row person because they did not answer all six questions about work stress). One of the disadvantages is that someone could answer just one question about work stress and still get a value. So you could set up a rule so that people have to answer at least half or more of the questions in order to calculate the mean work stress score:

egen b_depentmiss=rowmiss(b_depenth1 b_depenth2 b_depenth3 b_depenth4 b_depenth5 b_depenth6)

fre b_depentmiss

replace b_depenthmean =. if b_depentmiss >3 (this gets rid of four people who had four or more missing responses to the six work stress questions)

Comparing means

Now that we have a continuous job stress variable, we can look at differences in means by educational qualifications.

Table 6.8 clearly shows that the mean work stress decreases from degree qualifications to those with no qualifications. Comparing means works best if you are comparing the means of a continuous variable by levels of a categorical variable. It does not really work well if you are comparing the means of two continuous variables. Instead think of using a scatterplot or correlation.

What happens when you use a scatterplot with thousands of cases? It becomes not so easy to see a pattern unless there is a really strong correlation. One potential solution is to take a few random subsamples of the data set and run the scatterplots several times for each random subsample to see if you can observe an association between the two variables.

Table 6.8 Mean of the combined job stress measure by highest education qualification from wave 2 of Understanding Society

```
Summary for variables: b_depenthmean
        by categories of: b_hiqual_dv (Highest qualification, UKHLS & BHPS samples)
```

b_hiqual_dv	mean
Degree	1.828178
Other higher deg	1.817058
A-level etc	1.755063
GCSE etc	1.750003
Other qualificat	1.760992
No qualification	1.6535
Total	1.777502

Statistical tests to compare means and proportions

From the previous test, we can see that the means between educational qualification groups are different; however, we want to know how different they are. We can do this by using an analysis of variance (ANOVA) test (Table 6.9):

    oneway b_depenthmean b_hiqual_dv, tabulate

Table 6.9 Analysis of variance of the combined job stress measure by highest education qualification from wave 2 of Understanding Society

Highest qualificati on, UKHLS & BHPS samples	Summary of b_depenthmean		
	Mean	Std. Dev.	Freq.
Degree	1.8281776	.72661713	8,101
Other hig	1.8170576	.77144706	3,624
A-level e	1.7550635	.76256785	6,458
GCSE etc	1.7500028	.77792106	6,028
Other qua	1.7609924	.80030361	2,247
No qualif	1.6534998	.78550269	1,662
Total	1.7775024	.76273623	28,120

Analysis of Variance					
Source	SS	df	MS	F	Prob > F
Between groups	60.4519792	5	12.0903958	20.86	0.0000
Within groups	16298.242	28114	.579719784		
Total	16358.694	28119	.581766563		

Bartlett's test for equal variances: chi2(5) = 56.0855 Prob>chi2 = 0.000

The statistics provided are calculated for two groups. In STATA, these are called between groups and within groups. In other statistical packages, they may be called model and error or residuals. Between groups is the relationship between the independent variable (IV) and dependent variable (DV). Within groups is the remaining variation unaccounted for by the specified model.

The 'SS' is the sum of squares or the sum, across all observations, of the square differences of each observation from the overall mean. The 'df' is the degrees of freedom, which is the number of degrees of freedom associated with the sample variance. 'MS' is mean square or the sample variance which is SS/df. The 'F-test' tells you whether there is a relationship between the DV and IV based on the F distribution. This value is calculated dividing the mean square of the between groups by the mean square of the within groups. 'Prob>F' is the *p* value that the variation in the DV would be observed even if the IV was not associated with the DV. Bartlett's test for equal variances is used to test for one of the assumptions of ANOVAs, whether the variances are the same across groups. If the test is not significant, then ANOVAs are appropriate. Note that this test is sensitive to non-normal data, if your data is not normal then

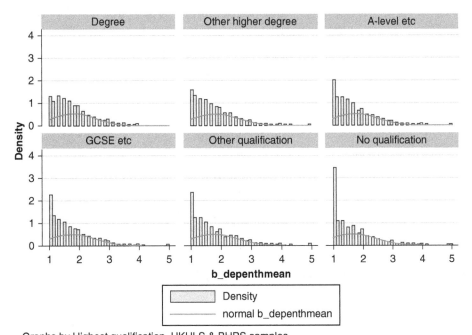

Graphs by Highest qualification, UKHLS & BHPS samples

Figure 6.3 Histogram of combined job stress measure by categories of highest education qualification

Note. GCSE = General Certificate of Secondary Education; UKHLS = UK Household Longitudinal Study; BHPS = British Household Panel Survey.

Table 6.10 Multiple comparison (Scheffé) analysis of variance of the combined job stress measure by highest education qualification from wave 2 of Understanding Society

Highest qualificati on, UKHLS & BHPS samples	Summary of b_depenthmean		
	Mean	Std. Dev.	Freq.
Degree	1.8281776	.72661713	8,101
Other hig	1.8170576	.77144706	3,624
A-level e	1.7550635	.76256785	6,458
GCSE etc	1.7500028	.77792106	6,028
Other qua	1.7609924	.80030361	2,247
No qualif	1.6534998	.78550269	1,662
Total	1.7775024	.76273623	28,120

Analysis of Variance

Source	SS	df	MS	F	Prob > F
Between groups	60.4519792	5	12.0903958	20.86	0.0000
Within groups	16298.242	28114	.579719784		
Total	16358.694	28119	.581766563		

Bartlett's test for equal variances: chi2(5) = 56.0855 Prob>chi2 = 0.000

Comparison of b_depenthm~n by Highest qualification, UKHLS & BHPS samples
(Scheffe)

Row Mean-Col Mean	Degree	Other hi	A-level	GCSE etc	Other qu
Other hi	-.01112 0.991				
A-level	-.073114 0.000	-.061994 0.009			
GCSE etc	-.078175 0.000	-.067055 0.004	-.005061 1.000		
Other qu	-.067185 0.018	-.056065 0.185	.005929 1.000	.01099 0.997	
No quali	-.174678 0.000	-.163558 0.000	-.101564 0.000	-.096503 0.001	-.107493 0.002

you may want to use a test that is less sensitive to data normality such as the Levene's test or the Browne–Forsythe test. If the test is significant, then you may want to use an alternative method for comparing means such as Kruskal–Wallis test which is a non-parametric test.

So what should you pay attention to? You need to look at the F-test and the Prob>F as well as the Bartlett's test or any other test of equal variance you may conduct. In the results above, we see that there is a relationship between the job stress and educational qualifications. However, according to the Bartlett's test, this model violates the assumption of equal variances among the groups. This is most likely due to non-normal data as seen in Figure 6.3:

histogram b_depenthmean, normal by(b_hiqual_dv)

If you would like to know the differences between the means of the groups, you need to include a multiple comparison test. In STATA, this is done by including the name of the test you want to use – Bonferroni, Scheffé or Šidák. Table 6.10 shows the output using Scheffé:

oneway b_depenthmean b_hiqual_dv, tabulate scheffe

Here you can see that there is no differences in the mean job stress level between the degree group and the higher education qualification group. There are also no differences in mean levels of job stress between A levels and General Certificate of Secondary Education (GCSE) or other qualifications groups or between GCSE and other qualifications groups. All other mean comparisons between groups are significant.

So to answer our research question, just looking at raw bivariate correlations, individuals with no qualifications have lower job stress scores than all individuals with higher qualifications. Individuals with a degree have more job stress scores than all other individuals, with the exception of those with other higher qualifications. While this answers our question, there may be some variables that we have not included in this relationship that may change our findings. Some examples would be job sector, age, gender or flexible working conditions. To examine whether and how these variables may alter this relationship, we would use multivariate modelling techniques.

Examining multivariate associations

Making statistical inference

Statistical inference is when we use data analysis to determine a probability distribution. In order to do this, we test hypotheses based on observed data or a sample that we assume is drawn from a population which we infer certain properties from. Because we are unable to know the true value of a population, we use statistics to estimate the uncertainty or sample to sample variation. Linear and logistic models, Cox models and Bayesian inference are just a few of the methods that can be used to determine statistical inference. The output from these statistics include but are not limited to parameter **estimates**, means, effect sizes, odds or rate ratios and probabilities.

To determine the degree of uncertainty, we usually use p values or confidence intervals (CIs) that are set to a specific level under which we would expect the same inferences to occur in other samples. Usually, we set this to 5% or 0.05. Therefore, if a p value is 0.02, then we would say that if the null hypothesis is true, there is a 2% chance of getting more extreme result than the one we observe. When using CIs, the standard practice is to use 95% CIs. When interpreting these numbers, you are saying that the range includes the plausible values of your parameter or that you are 95% confident that the true value of your sample lies within that range of numbers.

Inferential statistical tests on secondary data can be misused and misinterpreted. Sometimes, researchers may select an incorrect statistical test that does not reflect the underlying distribution of a variable. Researchers may also manipulate the data in order to find associations that are not there, this is called p-hacking.

For example, if data is not distributed normally, then a non-parametric test is required. Furthermore, the interpretation of p values is dependent on whether you are hypothesis testing or significance testing, and the results of tests of statistical significance are dependent upon sample size (Blume & Peipert, 2003, pp. 2–4). Thus, the results of inferential statistical tests cannot be taken at face value.

What is weighting? How do you use the derived weights?

Many secondary data sets provide weighting variables which are recommended to be used with any analyses of the data. However, despite their availability, it is common for many secondary analyses to ignore these weighting variables. This section describes what these weighting variables are, why it is important to use them in your analysis and how to use them.

Secondary data sets from surveys come from a sample of a population. Ideally, the sample in the data set is representative of the population it came from. In other words, the sample is representative in terms of all the variables measured in the survey. We would expect that the distribution of age, gender or ethnicity in the sample is similar to the distribution of the same variables in the population. However, this may not be the case because some groups are either over- or under-represented, either by the design of the study (survey design) or through **survey non-response** or self-selection into the sample (e.g. some groups of people are not willing to participate in the study). Not everyone in the population has an equal chance of being selected into the sample (unequal selection probabilities). Moreover, we know that even if the sample is chosen by a simple random sampling process, some people are less likely than others to agree to participate in surveys (which is often termed *non-response* *bias*). It is not advisable to treat the sample as a simple random sample from the population and ignore these factors that make the sample non-representative of the population. We need to correct for these factors in order to make reliable inferences from the survey. It is very rare for survey data to be collected using a simple random sampling design. Instead, more complicated sampling designs are often used, which means that unless these sampling designs are accounted for in the analysis, the point estimates and standard errors are likely to be wrong.

Perhaps the most common technique that is adopted to correct for representation is using a weighting adjustment. A weight is attached to each survey respondent (each row in the data). People who are under-represented in a survey get a probability weight larger than 1. So if women are under-represented, then they will have a probability weight that is larger than 1, so that when the weights are taken into account, the numbers of women are boosted. Conversely, people who are over-represented get a survey probability weight of less than 1, so that their numbers are reduced once the weights are applied.

In a secondary data set, there could be several types of weights that may be available for you as a researcher to use, so it is important to understand what the different weights mean. A sampling weight is a probability weight. A probability weight is the inverse of the probability of being included in the sample due to the sampling design. While many textbooks about statistical sampling tend to end their discussion of probability weights here, this definition does not fully describe the sampling weights that are included with actual survey data sets. Rather, the sampling weight, which is sometimes called the 'final weight', starts with the inverse of the sampling fraction, but then incorporates several other values, such as corrections for unit non-response, errors in the **sampling frame** (sometimes called non-coverage) and post-stratification. So a weighting variable can make several adjustments to the data; for example, it can simultaneously adjust for non-response and unequal selection probabilities.

Most large survey data sets include at least one weighting variable. Different weights may relate to different samples (e.g. a 'core' or 'ethnic boost' sample) or different sample units (e.g. individuals or households). An 'ethnic boost' sample oversamples people from ethnic minority backgrounds in order to overcome the problem of small sample sizes of some ethnic groups in samples from the general population. As some ethnic minority groups are oversampled in such 'ethnic boost' samples, the survey weight then assigns a survey probability weight of less than 1 to such people who are oversampled.

Grossing weights

Weights can also adjust a sample to make it look the same size as the population. These are called grossing weights. Grossing weights are useful when describing the prevalence of social phenomena in the population, such as incidences of crime. They are used in some official surveys, including the Crime Survey for England and Wales and the Labour Force Survey. When using grossing weights, results from data analysis will look like they come from a sample of millions, rather than a few thousand; thus, results can appear more precise than they might be in reality. As a result, some researchers prefer to rescale the weights to stop the artificial inflating of the sample size.

You need to use the weight for your results to reflect the population accurately. Some researchers prefer not to use these weights, but instead use other methods to avoid biases generated by the sampling process (e.g. by incorporating the sample selection process into the statistical model).

The details of any weights will be included in the survey documentation. It is important to read the documentation carefully to find out which weight to use for your analysis. The technical documentation from the deposited data must be read carefully to find out what kind of sampling design was used to collect the data. With many secondary data sets, the technical documentation can be quite extensive and sometimes even intimidating. There is usually a section or chapter called 'Sample Design', 'Variance Estimation' and so on. This is the part that tells you about the design elements included with the survey and how to use them. Some even give example code. If multiple sampling weights have been included in the data set, there will be some instruction about when to use which one. If there is a section or chapter on missing data or imputation, please read that. This will tell you how missing data were handled.

Several types of weights are provided in Understanding Society. We will be using one to see how means of job stress by educational qualification differ when unweighted or weighted.

Using the same code from the previous section for the ANOVA test,

```
oneway b_depenthmean b_hiqual_dv
```

This should get us the same table as in Table 6.9.

Next we run the same code but include our weighting variable **b_indscub_xw**:

```
oneway b_depenthmean b_hiqual_dv [w=b_indscub_xw]
```

From the results in Table 6.11, we can note a few things compared to Table 6.9. First, the means and standard deviations have changed. Next, the number of observations has also changed, this is due to some individuals having weights of 0.

Table 6.11 Weighted analysis of variance of the combined job stress measure by highest education qualification from wave 2 of Understanding Society

Highest qualificati on, UKHLS & BHPS samples	Summary of b_depenthmean			
	Mean	Std. Dev.	Freq.	Obs.
Degree	1.8299381	.72161194	7,888	7,908
Other hig	1.8109959	.76399942	3,551	3,560
A-level e	1.761243	.76174461	6,566	6,298
GCSE etc	1.7448886	.77938796	6,134	5,887
Other qua	1.7651406	.80808691	2,287	2,197
No qualif	1.6545636	.80530821	1,558	1,629
Total	1.7777139	.76261161	27,985	27,479

	Analysis of Variance				
Source	SS	df	MS	F	Prob > F
Between groups	56.7798872	5	11.3559774	19.59	0.0000
Within groups	15923.7783	27473	.579615562		
Total	15980.5582	27478	.58157647		

Bartlett's test for equal variances: chi2(5) = 103.9893 Prob>chi2 = 0.000

Sampling design elements include the sampling (or survey) weights, primary sampling units (PSUs) and strata. Not all secondary data provide all of these variables, but the key one to look out for is the sampling or survey weights.

PSU refers to the primary sampling unit or the first unit that is sampled in the survey design. For example, this could be the postcodes that were sampled from within larger districts and states. It is important to account for such clustering in the data (which means that people living in the sampled neighbourhoods have a much higher chance of being in the survey compared to people who are not living in the sampled neighbourhoods), otherwise the standard errors of any estimates in the analysis will be too small, leading to false positives when doing significance tests. Accounting for clustering in the data (using the PSUs) will tend to increase the standard errors.

Strata

Stratification is a method of breaking up the population into different groups, often by demographic variables such as gender, race or socio-economic status. Each individual in the population must belong to one, and only one, strata. Once the strata have been defined by the survey designers, samples are taken from each stratum as if it were independent of all of the other strata. This makes it cheaper to run surveys as you are sampling from within a much smaller group compared to the whole population.

Statistical programmes allow for identification of variables which identify the sampling design elements. In some programs, you will include these variables in the syntax of the models, for example, SAS. In other programs such as STATA, you will need to identify these variables first and then you can run subsequent analyses by using a keyword which indicates that these variables are to be taken into account.

Table 6.12 Survey weighted mean of the combined job stress measure by highest education qualification from wave 2 of Understanding Society

```
Survey: Mean estimation

Number of strata =    1,887          Number of obs    =     32,330
Number of PSUs   =    6,221          Population size =  27,985.26
                                     Design df        =      4,334

      Degree: b_hiqual_dv = Degree
   _subpop_2: b_hiqual_dv = Other higher degree
   _subpop_3: b_hiqual_dv = A-level etc
   _subpop_4: b_hiqual_dv = GCSE etc
   _subpop_5: b_hiqual_dv = Other qualification
   _subpop_6: b_hiqual_dv = No qualification
```

| | | Linearized | | |
Over	Mean	Std. Err.	[95% Conf. Interval]	
b_depenthmean				
Degree	1.829938	.0097756	1.810773	1.849103
_subpop_2	1.810996	.0146042	1.782364	1.839628
_subpop_3	1.761243	.0111662	1.739352	1.783134
_subpop_4	1.744889	.0120578	1.721249	1.768528
_subpop_5	1.765141	.0212562	1.723468	1.806814
_subpop_6	1.654564	.0250379	1.605476	1.703651

```
Note: 6 strata omitted because they contain no subpopulation
      members.
Note: Variance scaled to handle strata with a single sampling
      unit.
```

For example, if for wave 2 of Understanding Society, we would use the following code to indicate the survey sampling variables:

```
svyset psu [pweight= b_indinub_xw], strata(strata) singleunit
(scaled)
```

Let's examine whether the means produced earlier change using this code. We will then use the following code to produce means of job stress by educational qualifications:

```
svy: mean b_depenthmean, over(b_hiqual_dv)
```

where svy tells STATA to use and adjust the results according to the svyset statement. The results are shown in Table 6.12.

The means provided here are exactly the same as the weighted means from earlier; however, if you calculate the standard errors from the earlier table, you will see that the standard errors from the weighted-only calculations are smaller.

Basic longitudinal data analysis

Examples of longitudinal data

Longitudinal data collects information from the same individuals over time. Sometimes longitudinal studies collect data from a sample of people born in the same year or having some other common defining characteristic. These studies are called cohort studies. Cohort studies may collect data at seemingly random intervals or long intervals between data collections. Additionally, when there is attrition due to death or loss to follow-up, cohort studies do not bring in additional members to refresh their sample. Some examples of longitudinal cohort studies are the National Child Development Study (NCDS), Whitehall II Study, Millennium Cohort Study (MCS) and the 1970 British Birth Cohort Study.

When data are collected from a group of people at regular intervals, you have a panel study. Panel studies may, from time to time, add new members to maintain representativeness of their sample or to increase sample numbers. Understanding Society: UKHLS, the ELSA and the ONS LS are examples of panel studies.

Examining associations between variables measured at different times

Longitudinal data can be used to examine how an individual's circumstances change over time and what may predict those changes or what other changes or characteristics they are associated with. These circumstances may be individual, that is, educational attainment, labour force status, health status or relationship status, or can be related to more external factors such as household structure, parental health status or local or national governmental policy changes, just to name a few. Some of these changes in circumstances maybe rare and therefore harder to explore in general population samples such as, the diagnosis of cancer or moving house. In these cases, it may be difficult to explore research questions involving these events in longitudinal data sets with short follow-up periods. Some researchers choose to pool events across data collection waves and use other methods such as, including time variables to account for the longitudinal nature of the data. Other events may be more common – such as, birth of a child – or there is enough variation in the variable of interest among sample members – such as, attitudes towards household chores, for further exploration. You can then look at both short- and long-term associations with these factors.

Some examples of research conducted with longitudinal data include changes in school-leaving age on the educational attainment of young people, relationships between experiencing unemployment and well-being and use of social media and well-being among adolescents.

Describing change in a repeated measure

A major feature of longitudinal studies is the ability to ask respondents the same questions repeatedly. While repeated cross-sectional studies may ask the same questions, they are asked of different people and therefore we can only infer trends.

Modelling change in a repeated measure

There are several ways to model changes in repeated measures. Each of these methods comes with their own assumptions which you need to keep in mind in deciding which method to choose. The most common methods are the repeated measures ANOVA or repeated measures multivariate ANOVA (MANOVA) or general linear model (GLM), marginal multilevel models and mixed models. The ANOVA is used for univariate modelling, while repeated measures MANOVA and GLM can be used in multivariate modelling. These are quite simple models which are easy to interpret. However, they make many assumptions including the following:

1   The sample is a balance panel, that is, there are no observations with missing data.
2   There are equal correlations among the dependent variables, that is, the correlation between wave 1 and wave 2 is the same as the correlation between waves 1 and 5 or waves 1 and 9.

3   This can be problematic as more proximal, that is, closer, observations tend to be more closely correlated than observations that are further apart.

In a marginal multilevel model, the repeated outcomes are inserted in a multilevel schema, for example, level 1 is well-being and level 2 is time. Unlike repeated measures ANOVA, MANOVA or GLM, the marginal multilevel model does not assume equal correlation of the outcome variable. In fact, you can specify what type of correlation structure you wish to assign to the data or analysis you are conducting.

Mixed models are similar to marginal multilevel models in that they allow for correlation among outcome variables and specification of that correlation structure. However, mixed models add individual random effects to the model. Different levels of well-being of individuals at baseline or wave 1 is an example of a random effect. Multilevel models are able to control for this variation as well as other individual random effects observed in your data.

How you set up your data depends on what models you use to analyse your data. If you use repeated measures ANOVA, MANOVA or GLM, then your data needs to be in a wide format; however, if you use marginal multilevel or mixed models, then your data needs to be in a long format.

Practical longitudinal data analysis exercise

In this practical exercise, we will be examining how well-being changes when one becomes unemployed. We will use the first two waves of UKHLS for this exercise. The variables we will use are as follows:

Outcome Variable: b_scghq1_dv – Wave 2 GHQ-12 Likert Score

Independent Variable: a_jbstat – Wave 1 Employment Status

Control Variables: a_scghq1_dv, a_dvage, a_sex_dv, a_hiqual_dv, a_mastat_dv, a_ health a_disdif96, a_netinc1, a_hhnetinc3, a_hhsize, a_nkids_dv, a_tenure_dv – Wave 1 GHQ-12 Likert Score, age, gender, highest educational qualification, partnership status, limiting long-standing illness, income, household size, number of children in household and housing tenure

Data management

The first step to data analysis is creating a data set that contains all of the variables you will be using. This includes selecting those variables from potentially large data sets as well as examining them to ensure they are coded in a manner that will allow you to answer your research question. The following code will take the variables listed above which come from four different data sets, merge the data sets together and then create some new variables so that we can run our analyses.

Step 1: Merge wave 1 household and individual data sets.

*Read in household data set and keep the variables you want

```
use "file location\a_hhresp", clear
keep a_hidp a_hhnetinc3 a_hhsize a_nkids_dv a_tenure_dv a_ieqmoecd_dv
```

*Sort data set by identifying variable to merge with individual data set later

```
sort a_hidp
```

*Save data set to merge with individual data later

```
compress
save wave1_hh, replace
```

*Read in individual data set and keep variables you want

```
use "file location\a_indresp", clear
keep a_hidp pidp a_sex a_mastat_dv a_dvage a_racel_dv a_hiqual_dv a_jbstat a_
health a_disdif96 a_scghq1_dv a_netinc1 a_psu a_strata
```

*Sort data set by same identifying variable to merge with household data set

```
sort a_hidp
```

*Merge household data set into individual data set using the key identifying variable

```
merge a_hidp using wave1_hh
```

In STATA, when you merge data sets together, there is a _merge variable that is created. This is a three-category variable that tells you how many observations are in:

1   The number of observations that came from file 1 (in this case, a_indresp) but have no corresponding observations in file 2 (wave1_hh)
2   The number of observations that came from file 2 (in this example, wave1_hh) but have no corresponding observations in file 1 (in this example, a_indresp)
3   The number of observations found in both data sets (in this example, both a_indresp and wave1_hh)

For these analyses, we only want the observations from _merge to be equal to three:

```
tab _merge
keep if _merge==3
drop _merge
```

*Now we sort this data set by a different key identifying variable for when we want to merge with wave 2 as hidp number change from wave to wave in UKHLS

    sort pidp

*Save data set to merge with wave 2 data set later

    compress

    save wave1, replace

Step 2: Repeat previous steps for wave 2, note we are keeping slightly different variables from wave 1.

*Household level data

    use "file location\b_hhresp", clear

    keep b_hidp b_hhnetinc3 b_hhsize b_nkids_dv b_tenure_dv b_ieqmoecd_dv

    sort b_hidp

    compress

    save wave2_hh, replace

*Individual level data

    use "file location\b_indresp", clear

    keep b_hidp pidp b_jbstat b_scghq1_dv b_netinc1 b_indscus_lw

    sort b_hidp

    merge b_hidp using wave2_hh

    tab _merge

*Merge household and individual

    keep if _merge==3

    drop _merge

Step 3: Merge wave 1 data set with wave 2 data set.

    sort pidp

    merge pidp using wave1

*Again we only want the individuals who were present in both waves so we keep all observations where merge is equal to three.

    tab _merge

    keep if _merge==3

    drop _merge

Now that we have a data set that has both wave 1 and wave 2 data and includes only observations where individuals are present in both we can start with further sample restriction and creating new variables.

Step 4: Restrict the sample to those within working age 16 to 65 years and who are in employment (self or employed) at wave 1.

> drop if a_dvage <15
>
> drop if a_dvage >= 66
>
> keep if (a_jbstat==1 | a_jbstat==2)

Step 5: Recode and create new variables.

*Recoding selected variables so that missing codes are now set to '.'

> recode a_hhsize a_nkids_dv a_tenure_dv a_ieqmoecd_dv a_sex a_mastat_dv a_dvage a_racel_dv a_hiqual_dv a_jbstat a_health a_disdif96 a_scghq1_dv b_hhsize b_nkids_ dv b_tenure_dv b_ieqmoecd_dv b_jbstat b_scghq1_dv (-21/-1=.)

*Creating a 3-category employment status variable

> gen jbstat2_w2=a_jbstat
>
> recode jbstat2_w2 (1/2=1) (4 5 6 7 8 9 10 97=2) (3=3)

*Creating an adjusted household income variable

> gen adj_hhinc_w1=a_hhnetinc3/a_ieqmoecd_dv
>
> gen adj_hhinc_w2=b_hhnetinc3/b_ieqmoecd_dv

*Creating logged household and individual income variables

> gen nrmd_hhinc_w1 = ln(adj_hhinc_w1) if a_hhnetinc3 ~=(0/.)
>
> gen nrmd_hhinc_w2 = ln(adj_hhinc_w2) if b_hhnetinc3 ~=(0/.)
>
> gen nrmd_indinc_w1 = ln(a_netinc1) if a_netinc1 ~=(0/.)
>
> gen nrmd_indinc_w2 = ln(b_netinc1) if b_netinc1 ~=(0/.)

*Creating 3-category marital status variable

> gen partner_w1=a_mastat_dv
>
> recode partner_w1 (2/3=1) (10=1) (1=2) (4/9=3)

*Creating a 5-category ethnicity variable

> gen race_w1=a_racel_dv
>
> recode race_w1 (1/2=1) (9/11=2) (14/15=3) (3 4 12 13 16 17 97=4) (5/8=5)

*Creating a binary limiting long-standing illness variable

```
gen llti_w1=1 if a_health==1 & a_disdif96==0
replace llti_w1=1 if a_health==1 & a_disdif96==1
replace llti_w1=0 if a_health==2
```

*Rescoring GHQ so that higher scores indicate better well-being

```
gen ghq_l_w1=36-a_scghq1_dv
gen ghq_l_w2=36-b_scghq1_dv
```

*Creating a 3-category housing tenure variable

```
gen tenure_w1=a_tenure_dv
recode tenure_w1 (1/2=1) (6/7=2) (3 4 5 8=3)
```

Now that we have created all of the variables that we want to use in our analyses, we will give these new variables label names and values.

*Giving newly created variables labels

```
label variable race_w1 "Wave 1 Race/Ethnicity of Respondent"
label variable partner_w1 "Wave 1 Partnership Status of Respondent"
label variable llti_w1 "Wave 1 Limiting Long-term Illness"
label variable ghq_l_w1 "Wave 1 GHQ-12: Likert Scoring"
label variable ghq_l_w2 "Wave 2 GHQ-12: Likert Scoring"
label variable jbstat2_w2 "Wave 2 Current economic activity: 3 Category"
label variable nrmd_hhinc_w1 "Wave 1 Log Transformed Equivalised Net Household
Income"
label variable nrmd_indinc_w1 "Wave 1 Log Transformed Net Individual Income"
label variable nrmd_hhinc_w2 "Wave 2 Log Transformed Equivalised Net Household
Income"
label variable nrmd_indinc_w2 "Wave 2 Log Transformed Net Individual Income"
label variable tenure_w1 "Wave 1 Housing Tenure"
label define llsi      0 "No long-standing illness" ///
                       1 "Limiting Long-standing Illness"
label define jbst      1 "Employed: Yes" ///
                       2 "Economically Inactive" ///
                       3 "Employed: No"
label define ethn      1 "White British" ///
```

2 "Asian" ///

3 "Black African/Caribbean" ///

4 "Other" ///

5 "Mixed"

label define mstata   1 "Married/Cohabiting" ///

2 "Single" ///

3 "Other"

label define hstn   1 "Own" ///

2 "Private Rental" ///

3 "Other Rent and Accommodation"

*Assigning the new variables label values

label values llti_w1 llsi

label values jbstat2_w2 jbst

label values race_w1 ethn

label values partner_w1 mstata

label values tenure_w1 hstn

*Dropping variables that we no longer need for our analyses. This can help keep your data set small and clean.

drop b_jbstat a_hhnetinc3 b_hhnetinc3 a_ieqmoecd_dv b_ieqmoecd_dv a_netinc1 b_netinc1 b_hhnetinc3 a_mastat_dv a_racel_dv a_health a_disdif96 a_tenure_dv

Descriptive analysis

Now that we have these new variables we want to make sure they 'look' right and be able to describe them in our paper or report.

First, we will look at the categorical variables.

*Frequencies of categorical variables

tab1 a_sex race_w1 partner_w1 a_hiqual_dv llti_w1 tenure_w1

Next, we will have a look at the continuous variables.

*Means of selected continuous variables

sum a_dvage ghq_l_w1 nrmd_hhinc_w1 nrmd_indinc_w1 a_hhsize a_nkids_dv

We will ignore some variables such as a_psu, a_strata and b_indscus_lw as these are variables that we will use in our regression analyses to control for survey design but do not need to describe.

Rather than show you each of these outputs individually, I have put the results into a table (see Table 6.13).

Table 6.13 Descriptive statistics of socio-demographic characteristics at Understanding Society wave 1

Characteristic	N	%
Gender (men)	9925	49
Ethnicity		
White British	15,745	80
Asian	1474	8
Black African/Caribbean	869	4
Other	1226	6
Mixed	334	2
Partnership status		
Married/cohabiting	14,726	73
Single	3520	17
Other	1915	10
Highest educational qualification		
Degree	6016	30
Other higher	2722	14
A level	4101	20
GCSE	4239	21
Other qualification	1653	8
No qualification	1415	7
Limiting long-standing illness	5106	26
Housing tenure		
Own	15,187	76
Private rental	2,568	13
Other rent and accommodation	2,359	12
	M	SD
GHQ-12 Score	25.36	4.72
Age	41.79	11.65
Logged household income	7.28	0.56
Number of children in household	0.73	1.00

Note. GCSE = General Certificate of Secondary Education; GHQ = General Health Questionnaire.

This is one example of how to create a descriptive table. We include all of our socio-demographic characteristic variables and other **control variables** from wave 1. A short write-up of this table would look something like the following.

The analytical sample was 49% male and a majority white British, 80%. More than 70% of the sample was married or cohabiting, with 17% single and 10% have previously been partnered. Almost one third of the sample had obtained a degree (30%), with GCSE (21%) and A levels (20%), as the next largest educational qualification groups. Only 7% of the sample had no qualifications. The vast majority of the sample lived in homes they owned (76%). Twenty-six percent of the sample reported having a limiting long-standing illness. The mean age of the sample was 41.76 years (SD = 11.65). The mean logged household income was 7.28 (SD = 0.56) and the average household had less than one child, mean = 0.73, SD = 1.00. A mean of 0.73 children in the household indicates many households had no children. The mean GHQ score was 25.36 (SD = 4.72) indicating a relatively low level of anxiety and distress among this sample.

Regression analysis

Our final step is to run a linear regression analysis. We will be regressing the outcome variable, GHQ-12 score at wave 2 on our independent variable Employment status at wave 2. We will then be including a number of covariate variables that we believe are related to the outcome variable but we want to exclude their effects from our relationship between the dependent (i.e. y or outcome variable) and the independent (i.e. x) variables. Note that we are controlling for the GHQ-12 score at wave 1, which enables us to draw different conclusions compared to cross-sectional data. By controlling for baseline GHQ-12, we are in effect examining predictors of change in GHQ-12 from wave 1 to 2.

UKHLS is a survey that uses complex sampling and because it is longitudinal it can suffer from attrition. Thus, we will use STATA's svy command, which allows us to control for the sampling design, and we can use weights to estimate this relationship.

*The first statement tells STATA that we are setting our data to use their svy commands.

svyset a_psu [pweight= b_indscus_lw], strata(a_strata) singleunit(scaled)

*This statement is our regression model. The ib#. tells STATA to create dummy variables, where the '#' indicates the category that we want to use as the reference category. In the case of binary variables such as *llti*, we only use i and since the variable is 0/1 STATA will automatically use 0 as the reference category.

svy: regress ghq_l_w2 ib1.jbstat2_w2 ib1.a_sex a_dvage ib1.race_w1 ib1.partner_w ib1.a_hiqual_dv i.llti_w1 ib1.tenure_w1 nrmd_hhinc_w1 a_nkids_dv ghq_l_w1

Again, rather than show the STATA output, we put the results into Table 6.14, which you may see in a report or paper.

Table 6.14   Parameter estimates from the regression model of GHQ-12

Estimate	β	95% Confidence Interval
Employment status (Ref = employed)		
Economically inactive	−0.69	[−1.11, −0.27]
Unemployed	−2.38	[−3.05, −1.71]
Gender (Ref = men)		
Women	−0.54	[−0.70, −0.39]
Age	0.002	[−0.007, 0.01]
Ethnicity (Ref = white British)		
Asian	−0.16	[−0.57, 0.25]
Black African/Caribbean	0.59	[0.08, 1.10]
Mixed	0.31	[−0.36, 0.98]
Other	−0.02	[−0.39, 0.35]
Partnership status (Ref = married/cohabiting)		
Single	0.28	[0.03, 0.53]
Previously partnered	−0.09	[−0.38, 0.19]
Highest educational qualification (Ref = degree)		
Other higher	−0.020	[−0.26, 0.22]
A level	0.00	[−0.23, 0.22]
GCSE etc.	0.11	[−0.11, 0.34]
Other qualification	−0.02	[−0.32, 0.27]
No qualification	0.32	[−0.07, 0.70]
Limiting long-standing illness (Ref = no limiting long-standing illness)		
Limiting long-standing illness	−0.82	[−1.02, −0.62]
Housing tenure (Ref = own)		
Private rental	−0.19	[−0.46, 0.07]
Other rental and accommodation	−0.45	[−0.73, −0.17]
Logged household income	0.34	[0.19, 0.50]
Number of children in household	−0.05	[−0.14, 0.04]
Wave 1 GHQ score	0.46	[0.44, 0.48]

Note. β = parameter estimate; Ref = reference; GHQ = General Health Questionnaire.

We would write up the findings as follows.

The results of this model show that compared to participants who were employed at wave 2, those who were unemployed on average had GHQ-12 score that was 2.38 points lower, 95% CI = [−3.05, −1.71]. This indicates poorer well-being. While participants who were economically inactive (i.e. retired, long-term sick, training, etc.) also had lower GHQ-12 scores, $\beta = -0.69$, 95% CI = [−1.11, −0.27] compared to those who remained employed, they were not as low as those for the unemployed. Women had lower GHQ-12 scores than men by 0.54 points, 95% CI = [−0.70, −0.39]. Compared to married or cohabiting participants, single participants had higher GHQ-12 scores, $\beta = 0.29$, 95% CI = [0.03, 0.53]. There was no difference in GHQ-12 scores between previously partnered participants and married or cohabiting participants, $\beta = -0.09$, 95% CI = [−0.38, 0.19]. Participants with a limiting long-standing illness had lower levels of well-being than those with no illness, $\beta = -0.82$, 95% CI = [−1.02, −0.62]. As income increased, GHQ-12 scores also increased, $\beta = 0.34$, 95% CI = [0.19, 0.50]. A similar pattern was seen with wave 1 GHQ-12 scores where higher scores at wave 1 were associated with higher scores at wave 2, $\beta = 0.46$, 95% CI = [0.44, 0.48]. There were no associations with age, highest educational qualifications or number of children in the household.

So what is the answer to the research question? When controlling for a number of covariates, we see that being unemployed is associated with poorer well-being compared to those who were employed.

Have a look in Appendix 1 for another example of some data analyses and the reporting of results from the UK Household Longitudinal Study, this time using the biomarker data in that dataset.

Chapter Summary

- Often the data you get from data archives are not immediately suitable for statistical analysis. These variables may be in the 'raw' form – direct answers to questions and need to be transformed into something more meaningful for analysis.
- The key is to not over-manipulate or torture the data in order to get the results you want. You should make sure to have very clear research questions, hypotheses and data strategies prior to starting your data analyses.
- One relatively minor way to manipulate the data is to recode the missing values for the variables of interest. Another way of manipulating data is to combine response categories. Often researchers use a mixture of both to determine whether they should reduce category numbers.
- When generating new variables there are a few simple things to remember:
  - Use meaningful variable names.
  - Use value and variable labels.

- When creating cross tabulations, it may be easier to recode your key variables into binary variables. This is because 2 × 2 tables are easier to read and understand than larger tables. When generating binary variables (0/1) use 1 to indicate the event or concept you are interested in.
- Statistical inference is when we use data analysis to determine a probability distribution. In order to do this, we test hypotheses based on observed data or a sample that we assume is drawn from a population which we infer certain properties from.
- To determine the degree of uncertainty, we usually use p values or CIs that are set to a specific level under which we would expect the same inferences to occur in other samples.

Further Reading

Longhi, S., & Nandi, A. (2020). *A practical guide to using panel data*. Sage.

Rabe-Hesketh, S., & Skrondal, A. (2012). *Multilevel and longitudinal modeling using Stata* (3rd ed.). Stata Press.

7

WRITING UP YOUR ANALYSES

TARANI CHANDOLA AND CARA BOOKER

Chapter Overview

Background 108

Existing guidelines 108

Reporting your results in words 110

Preparing tables 111

Preparing graphs 111

Practical exercise 112

Further Reading 117

Background

It is really important to clearly write up the results of your analyses. Unfortunately, there are a lot of analyses which are poorly written up, which then makes it really hard for a reader to understand what analyses were done by the researcher and also whether they can make some valid inferences from the analyses.

This chapter will provide some guidelines for reporting your secondary data analyses.

Existing guidelines

There are several guidelines which may be used to structure research papers and reports for different types of studies. For example, the CONSORT (Consolidated Standards of Reporting Trials) guidelines (www.consort-statement.org) are used to structure reporting of randomised trials, and the PRISMA (Preferred Reporting Items for Systematic Reviews and Meta-Analyses) guidelines (www.prisma-statement.org) are used to structure systematic reviews. Reporting of observational studies, such as UKHLS, should follow the structure outlined by STROBE (Strengthening the Reporting of Observational studies in Epidemiology) guidelines (www.strobe-statement.org). STROBE guidelines are to be used with three specific types of observational research: cohort, case–control and cross-sectional studies.

Incomplete and inadequate reporting of research results in an inability to adequately assess the strengths and weaknesses of studies reported in the social science, epidemiology and medical literature. It is important to understand what was planned or unplanned, what was done, what was found and what the results mean. Many journals recommend the following of these guidelines because they can improve the quality of reporting and increase possible replication or reproducibility.

Many of the guidelines in the STROBE checklist are relevant for secondary data analysis, although not all the recommended guidelines will be relevant to social scientists as they are primarily written for medical researchers. Some recommendations suggest being explicit about the design of the study in the title of the paper or report of the analysis. For example, you could mention whether the analysis is based on cross-sectional or longitudinal data. You could also mention the names of the data set you are analysing, either in the title or in the abstract of the paper or report. Other recommendations are to specify the research hypotheses and justify them based on the existing theory or evidence. When reporting the methods used in the study, it is important to include details about the settings and relevant dates of the data collection, who the participants were in the sampling frame and how they were sampled. It is also important to clearly describe all the variables in the analysis, whether these are your key variables of interest (the independent and dependent variables) or your control variables. If you use derived variables, you should indicate how they were created. All the variables in the analyses should typically have been established to be valid and reliable. You would normally refer to previous literature showing how the variables (or combinations of variables) relate to your concept of interest in the sampled population. If this has not been done before, you may need to establish the validity of the variables you use for the analysis, especially if these are variables that have not been used in the literature before. If you recode a variable into different groups, you need to provide a justification for this transformation. It is really important to have a section describing the statistical methods you are using. This includes how you plan to go from descriptive statistical methods to inferential statistics. This is especially necessary if you plan on making causal inferences from observed associations; you will need to describe what statistical methods you will use to address the problems of making causal inferences from observed associations. It is also important to describe any missing data in the analysis and how you intend to address the problem of making inferences from secondary data with a large proportion of missing data. If you analyse a subset of the participants in the secondary data, you will need to describe why and how this selection of the subset occurred.

When describing the results of your analyses, it is important to describe the distribution of the variables you use (using measures of central tendency and dispersion). When you have a dependent variable to analyse, you could also show how the mean of the dependent variable changes by levels of the independent variables and covariates. This gives the reader some idea about the overall pattern of associations between the key variables in your analysis. If you have missing data, it is also important to show what proportion of your sample is missing for each variable. If you use regression models, you could show how the estimates (and 95% CIs) of the association change when you enter control variables into the model. Also, it is useful not just to report the relative risk measures (e.g. odds ratios) but also to translate them into predicted values of the dependent variable by levels of your independent variables.

When discussing your results, you should refer back to your original research questions and summarise what your key findings were in relation to those questions. Any limitations of the study, especially in terms of potential biases in the data, measurements or analysis, need to be discussed. It is useful to frame this discussion in terms of the direction and magnitude of potential biases. For example, is the limitation of the data (e.g. missing data) a large problem? If this is not a serious problem, then you could argue that although there are some missing data in the analysis, this is unlikely to substantially change the overall pattern of your results. You could also go further and illustrate how you think the direction of the bias would go. For example, if you have fewer people with low education in your analysis (because they refused to take part in the survey) as well as fewer unhealthy people (as sick people tended not to take part), then you may be able to argue that the correlation between education and health could potentially be stronger if the missing people with low education and poor health were in the sample you analysed. It is also useful to discuss how generalisable your study results are and whether you can make any inferences back to the population the secondary data comes from.

Reporting your results in words

As noted in chapter 6, there are issues with use of p values in determining statistical inference. Similar issues occur when reporting statistical significance or the results of a statistical analysis. There are alternatives that could be used when reporting results. One method is to report the effect size. Reporting effect sizes gives the reader context to the figures presented in tables or figures. Instead of writing, 'Financial stress was significantly associated with depression', it would be better to highlight

- the scale and direction of the association and/or
- the size of the effect.

For example, from the results in Table 6.14, the regression coefficient from unemployment is –2.38. We could have a 95% CI of [–3.05, –1.71]. A poor way to write this would be 'Becoming unemployed was significantly associated with a lower GHQ-12 score compared to staying employed'. A better way to say this would be 'Becoming unemployed was associated with a 2.38-point decrease in GHQ-12 score. This is the equivalent of 0.5 of a standard deviation'.

Try to summarise your tables using text. This text should not just repeat the information presented in the table but also should give context to the size of the effect and/or the direction of the association.

Many statistical tests are influenced by sample size. One way of reporting misleading statistics is when percentages are used to report the findings for small sample sizes. For example, when 19 out of 20 respondents answer 'yes', the percentage is 95%. In order to get 95% in a sample of 1,000 people, you require 950 'yes' answers. The validity of the percentage is not the same between the two samples, and providing only the percentage change without the full context regarding sample size may mislead the reader to make assumptions that are incorrect.

Preparing tables

Tables should be self-explanatory. The reader should not need to read the text to understand the figures in the table. Tables should have a clear title that explains the data contained within. The data should be laid out in a clear manner. Descriptive tables should include information about all the variables included in the analyses but not about variables that are not included. If you are going to stratify your analysis, for example, run separate models for males and females, you may want to provide descriptive statistics by gender. If you make any comparisons within the descriptive table, include test statistics. For example, if you are comparing mean age between men and women in the table, you will conduct a t test, and you can include the CIs or the p values in the test to let the reader know if these means are different from each other.

Tables that contain results from statistical models should have clear titles and all the relevant information. Make sure to include reference groups, estimates and levels of uncertainty for independent variables. Clearly delineate whether the estimates are adjusted or not. You may want to provide sample sizes, either in the title or within the table. Where appropriate, you may want to include fit statistics (e.g. those used in structural equation modelling) or R squared (i.e. how well the regression fits the data). You may want to include estimates and levels of uncertainty of control variables in the tables; however, if you do not, make sure you include your control variables in a table footnote. Finally, include definitions of any acronyms used in the table, define units (where necessary) and mention whether you utilised weights in your models.

Preparing graphs

Use of graphs and charts is a very effective way of providing your results in a visual manner; however, care must be taken in how you present the data visually. All charts and graphs must include the scale used, the starting value (i.e. 0 or other) and the method of calculation (e.g. data set and time period). Some common data visualisation mistakes include using the wrong graphs, using improper graphs which are impossible (e.g. using pie graphs or stacked charts with data that does not add up to 100) and including too much information on one graph. Remember that just because a graph may look fun or cool does not mean that the reader will be able to fully understand the data or what you are trying to convey. Be sure to identify intermediate data points and add context to increase understanding. If you are using data from different sources, data sets, times, locations and so on, be sure to use best practices for comparisons or inclusions on the same graphs or charts.

Practical exercise

Use this small data set that is a very small subsample ($n = 25$) of four variables taken from one of the waves of Understanding Society (Table 7.1). The four variables are age (Age), sex (Sex), household income (HH_income) and highest educational qualifications (Quals). Let's imagine that you are interested in finding out which variables are associated with household income. What should you do first? How will you go about presenting the descriptive statistics?

Table 7.1 Subsample ($n = 25$) of four variables taken from one of the waves of Understanding Society

ID	Age	Sex	HH_income	Quals
1	58	Male	832.3	Other qualifications
2	77	Male	1360.4	No qualifications
3	75	Male	1871.8	Degree
4	35	Male	2138.7	Degree
5	41	Male	1489.9	GCSE, etc.
6	—	—	—	—
7	51	Female	688.4	GCSE, etc.
8	—	—	—	—
9	32	Female	970.9	Degree
10	67	Female	699.6	No qualifications
11	—	—	—	—
12	64	Female	1075.4	Other higher qualifications
13	—	—	—	—
14	71	Female	897.0	GCSE, etc.
15	—	—	—	—
16	—	—	—	—
17	68	Female	3417.2	Degree
18	48	Male	2078.6	A level, etc.
19	20	Female	601.0	A level, etc.
20	28	Female	518.5	A level, etc.
21	39	Female	1135.4	A level, etc.
22	59	Female	2197.1	Degree
23	—	—	—	—
24	32	Male	1045.6	Degree
25	39	Female	1332.7	A level, etc.

Note. GCSE = General Certificate of Secondary Education.

One of the first things you notice about this particular data set is that there are a few people with missing data. Seven people out of 25 (or 28%) have no data. This requires some investigation and explanation. Usually, you would refer back to the survey documentation about why these particular people had no data. At other times, you would examine other variables in the data set for reasons for the missing data. Sometimes, there could be a simple explanation – such as the missing data was due to that particular person not being sampled at that specific wave but at a future wave. This is actually the reason for the missing data on the seven people in the above data set. However, it could also be that the reason for the missing data is that six people who were part of the Understanding Society sample at an earlier wave had decided not to participate in this wave. This is a more problematic situation as you would need to examine the reasons why people are dropping out of the survey. If dropping out of the survey is a non-random process, then any inferences you make based on a data set with a lot of missing data could be biased.

Our main variable of interest is household income, and we can clearly see that this is a continuous variable. It would make sense to use a histogram to examine the distribution of this variable (Figure 7.1). If you are using STATA, you can use the command

histogram HH_income

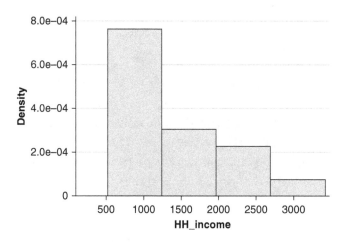

Figure 7.1 Histogram of household income

We can immediately see that the distribution of household income is highly skewed, with most households earning between £500 and £1000 in a month and very few households earning £3000 or more a month.

It would also be useful to present some descriptive statistics for these data. We can use some of the commands in a statistical package like STATA to provide these descriptive statistics. For example, tabstat HH_income , by(Quals) stat(n mean sd)

will produce a table as shown in Table 7.2.

Table 7.2 STATA output from tabstat command

```
          Summary for variables: HH_income
            by categories of: Quals


       Quals |        N      mean        sd
   ----------+------------------------------
           . |        0         .         .
   A-level et |        5  1133.24   631.4031
      Degree |        6  1940.217   897.9375
     GCSE etc |        3   1025.1   415.8218
   No qualifi |        2     1030   467.2562
   Other high |        1   1075.4         .
   Other qual |        1    832.3         .
   ----------+------------------------------
       Total |       18  1352.806   742.8125
```

However, that does not look like an easy table to understand. So it is useful to edit the table so that it is easier to read. You can do this by hand, within the STATA package itself (there are special commands to help prepare tables), or you could use a spreadsheet programme like Excel. Table 7.3 is one example of what a descriptive table could look like, which was prepared by copying and pasting the results from the STATA output in Table 7.2 into Excel and then editing the results in Excel.

Table 7.3 Mean and standard deviation (*SD*) of household income by highest qualifications and sex

	n	*M*	*SD*
Highest qualifications			
Degree	6	1940.2	897.9
Other higher qualifications	1	1075.4	.
A-level or higher	5	1133.2	631.4
GCSE qualifications	3	1025.1	415.8

	n	M	SD
Other qualifications	1	832.3	.
No qualifications	2	1030.0	467.3
Sex			
Female	11	1230.3	861.2
Male	7	1545.3	506.4
Total	18	1352.8	742.8

Note. GCSE = General Certificate of Secondary Education.

Remember to include the sample size (*n*) in your descriptive table. And also make sure you spell out any abbreviations in the table. As Age is a continuous variable, you could group (or recode) Age into meaningful age categories and add in the descriptive statistics of HH_income (*n*, mean and *SD*) to Table 7.3. Or you could also examine the scatter plot of Age and HH_income (Figure 7.2). The STATA command is

twoway (scatter Age HH_income)

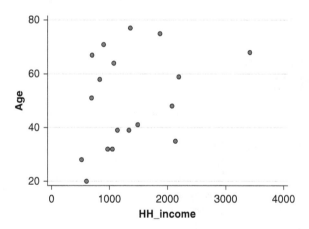

Figure 7.2 Scatter plot of Age and HH_income

We can see that there is some positive correlation between age and household income. On average, older people tend to have higher levels of household income. However, there are a few issues with the graph as it is. Firstly, the units of age and household income are not displayed, which makes it hard to understand how the two variables are related. Another potential problem is that HH_income is on the *x*-axis. Normally, we would have the dependent variable on the *y*-axis. As age cannot be the dependent variable (household income cannot 'cause' how old you are or when you were born), we would normally have household income plotted on the *y*-axis. We can rerun the graph (Figure 7.3) using the following STATA command:

twoway (scatter HH_income Age), ytitle(household income (£ per month)) xtitle(Age (years))

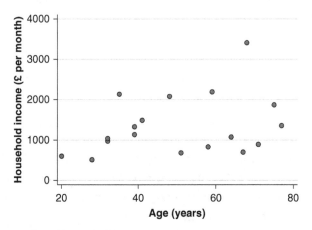

Figure 7.3 Scatter plot of household income and age

Remember to always include a title for your tables and graphs that explains to the reader what the tables or graphs are about.

Chapter Summary

- Incomplete or inadequate reporting of research results in an inability to adequately assess the strengths and weaknesses of studies reported in the social science, epidemiology and medical literature.
- When reporting the methods used in a study, it is important to include details about the settings and relevant dates of the data collection, who the participants were in the sampling frame and how they were sampled.
- It is also important to clearly describe all the variables in the analysis, both your key variables of interest (the independent and dependent variables) and your control variables. If you are using derived variables, you should indicate how they were created.
- When describing the results of your analyses, it is important to describe the distribution of the variables you use (using measures of central tendency and dispersion).
- When discussing your results, you should refer back to your original research questions and summarise what your key findings were in relation to those questions. Any limitations of the study, especially in terms of potential biases in the data, measurements or analysis, need to be discussed.
- It is also useful to discuss how generalisable your study results are and whether you can make any inferences back to the population the secondary data comes from.
- Tables should be self-explanatory. The reader should not need to read the text to understand the figures in the table.
- All charts and graphs must include the scale used, the starting value (i.e. 0 or other) and the method of calculation (e.g. data set and time period).

Further Reading

Vandenbroucke, J. P., von Elm, E., Altman, D. G., Gøtzsche, P. C., Mulrow, C. D., Pocock, S. J., Poole, C., Schlesselman, J. J., & Egger, M. (2007). Strengthening the Reporting of Observational Studies in Epidemiology (STROBE): Explanation and elaboration. *PLOS Medicine*, *4*(10), e297. https://doi.org/10.1371/journal. pmed.0040297

Wasserstein, R. L., Schirm, A. L., & Lazar, N. A. (2019). Moving to a world beyond '$p < 0.05$'. *The American Statistician*, *73*(Suppl. 1), 1–19. https://doi.org/10.1080/0 0031305.2019.1583913

8

COMPLEXITIES OF WORKING WITH SECONDARY DATA: LIMITATIONS OF ARCHIVAL AND SECONDARY DATA ANALYSIS

TARANI CHANDOLA

Chapter Overview

Background 120

Identifying problems and limitations in secondary data 120

Using derived variables 122

Dealing with missing data 123

Changing your research questions... 126

Showing critical awareness... 127

Sharing your analyses and coding... 128

Further Reading 129

Background

The availability of research data sets through data archives and the increasing ease by which such data can be analysed through statistical software packages mean that it is becoming easier for people to make errors when analysing data. These errors could arise from a secondary researcher's unfamiliarity with the research data, or they could be related to incorrect inferences being made from the data. This chapter identifies some common mistakes some secondary researchers make and what we can do to reduce the chances of making such mistakes.

Identifying problems and limitations in secondary data

One of the biggest limitations of using secondary data is that you are limited to the data that is already collected. So when your papers or reports are being reviewed, you may be asked questions about why you did not use a particular variable or concept in your analysis and the reason will often be that the data was not collected.

There are some things you could do to mitigate against the lack of appropriate data in your secondary data set. The first is to ask the people who deposited the data whether there are additional variables that were not deposited in the archive which you could access. Very often, sensitive and personal data are not released to data archives because of the risk of identifying individuals. However, it may be possible to obtain such data provided the data collector or depositor is satisfied that you are a bona fide researcher and that there is a low risk of individuals being identified with the release of their personal data. Sometimes the data collector or depositor will be satisfied with additional checks on your researcher status (e.g. whether you are in academia) and your research proposal, and will require you to sign additional documentation to guard against the release of personal and sensitive data. Sometimes the additional data will only be released to you as a researcher if you agree to analyse the data in a secure environment. This is especially true when you are requesting for additional data linked to individuals. These secure environments vary considerably, from a room in an office without access to the internet, where data can only be brought in or taken out under supervision, to a secure room in the data depositor's office.

At other times, you may be able to link in data from other data sets at an aggregate level, such as at a country, regional or district level. There may be published data at the area levels that may be relevant for the secondary data you are using, so it may be possible to link in data from other sources of secondary data. There may be times when the identifier for an area is not available. This is especially true of small areas, as there is an increased risk of identifying individuals when you know in which area they live. Some data depositors may be willing to link in small-area data that you require to their individual-level data. As they do the linkage themselves, there is a lower risk that this linkage could result in the identifying of individuals than if they release the data and give you the small-area identifiers alongside the individual-level data. This linkage may come at some cost, as asking for such bespoke linkages takes up resources for the data depositor.

Sometimes when you don't have the specific variables you are interested in, you may be able to make do with proxy or related variables that are similar to your variable of interest. However, there are large disciplinary differences in terms of what can be considered a **proxy variable**. For example, for many health researchers, years in education is often used as a proxy measure for socioeconomic status, whereas status for sociologists would often require a finer-grained measure that is validated to measure the concept in a specific population.

Another type of data that is often useful for secondary analysis but is often not available in data archives is paradata. This is data on the data collectors themselves and the process of data collection. For example, you may be interested in the gender of the interviewer of a survey, or the time of day or spatial location of the interview. As these data can possibly lead to the identifying of individuals, it is rare for such data to be released to data archives, but you can ask the data depositors about the possibility of obtaining such paradata should such data be a key focus of your research.

Another pitfall of secondary data analysis is that the most interesting research questions may already have been analysed and reported. Typically, the data collectors would have reported and published their key findings from the data before you, as a secondary data analyst, get a chance to use their data. However, this should not put you off as the data deposited is often very rich in detail, and it is very unlikely that the data collectors would have analysed and reported on all the interesting research questions. Furthermore, you may have alternative methodological approaches to use on the secondary data set which have not been tried before. Also, you may wish to use a combination of secondary data sets to answer your research question, and the combination of secondary data is something that the data collectors of a specific data set have not done before.

Another key limitation of secondary data is that you cannot collect further data on the sample, at least for that particular time and place. This means that your sample size for analysis is restricted, and it may be that you cannot investigate smaller groupings within the secondary data because of the small sample sizes. This is especially true when you wish to investigate the interactions between different groups within your secondary data. For example, it is well known that it is hard to collect data on a number of ethnic minorities from representative samples of the population because of the small numbers of some minorities. This makes it hard for a secondary data analyst to investigate those small ethnic minority groups in their analyses. Someone who collects primary data would purposefully sample additional ethnic minority groups if ethnicity is their key research question. However, a secondary data analyst is limited to the sample sizes of the groups in their data. Some researchers have overcome this problem by combining different data sets together so as to increase the sample size of small ethnic groups. This works best when the data sets being combined are part of a series, such as the HSE. As the data sets have a common methodological framework and a common underlying population (albeit at different time points), it can make intuitive sense to merge two consecutive years of a cross-sectional study like the HSE to have a larger sample size.

Another problem that you could encounter during your secondary data analysis is that your results may not match the published set of results in a report or journal article. This can often happen for many reasons. You may have made a mistake, in which case you can check your analysis again. It may have been that you used a different subset of the analytical sample compared to the analysis in the published literature. Or it could also have been that the methods you used were different from the ones in the literature. A typical example would be when you or the literature does not use the appropriate weighting methods (such as the use of survey **weights**), if these have already been derived by the data depositors. It could also be that the people who published the literature made a mistake. So it is really important to go through their descriptive statistics tables to see if they have the same number and groups of people in their analysis as in yours.

Using derived variables

Data depositors who make good-quality secondary data sets available in data archives prepare their data well for use by other researchers. They know that there are some common variables that nearly all researchers could benefit from and prepare derived variables so that they can be used by secondary data analysts.

The benefit of using variables already derived by the data depositor is that it gives you some reassurance that the complexity of data that goes into deriving a particular variable for analysis is checked and quality checked. As derived variables are based on summaries of other variables, often with complex question routings, recodes and loops, it is often not so easy to derive these variables yourself. A typical example is to derive the highest educational qualification that a person has. If the survey directly asks a person, 'What is your highest educational qualification?' and asks them to choose an option from a range of options, we would not need to derive this variable. However, for some people, this question is not so easy to answer as there are some vocational qualifications that are not so easy to rank against academic qualifications.

Similarly, people who have educational qualifications from other countries often do not find it easy to rank their qualifications against the qualifications listed in a survey as they may be unfamiliar with those qualifications. So rather than getting the survey respondent to rank their qualifications, surveys often ask detailed questions about all the qualifications someone has obtained. Once they have all those data and related variables, the data collectors then try to rank the different qualifications and group them into a single variable with just a few categories, to make it easier for secondary researchers to use this as a variable rather than having to deal with examining each qualification in detail and making a judgement call about whether a particular qualification is higher or lower than the next one.

Once the data collector or depositor has derived the variable, they often publish how they have derived this variable when they release the data to archives. This can typically be part of the data documentation they publish alongside the data. For a secondary data analyst, it is really recommended to work with these derived data – partly because this helps you to summarise complex data in a reliable and validated way but also because it gives you an insight into the key variables that the original data collectors were working with. Having an insight into what were the main motivations for conducting the original data collection could help you as a secondary data analyst in your research. For example, even if you are not interested in using the derived variable as an independent or dependent variable in a regression model, you could consider using it as a 'control' variable, partly because the data collectors thought that this variable is of importance to their research.

As an exercise to get familiar with the data set, it can be useful to follow the code or the method by which the data depositor has derived a particular variable. You should get the same distribution of the variable you derive by yourself as you would if you used the variable already derived by the data depositor.

Dealing with missing data

All social data sets have to deal with the problem of missing data. If the data is from a survey, typically there will be some people who do not respond to the survey (unit non-response), and even if someone does take part in an interview or questionnaire, they may not answer all the questions (item non-response). As a secondary data analyst, it is not so easy to find out the reasons why some of the data is missing, mainly because you often lack detailed information about the participant or about the specific data collection process for that participant. However, it is possible that such missing information could have an impact on the substantive inferences you make from the data. So it is always important to examine the reasons why some of the data is missing and explore what are some of the methods to compensate for the missing data.

First of all, it is important to distinguish between three types of mechanisms that result in missing data. The first is the *missing completely at random* (MCAR) mechanism. This is a random process that results in missing data in your data set. Say, for example, that a random file of the interviews from a survey was damaged and all the data from those interviews was lost from the data set – this could be an MCAR process. Although you would lose some members of the targeted sample of interviewees (and hence lose statistical power to detect significant differences), you could still analyse the data on the people that you have in the data set and make correct inferences, because it was a random process that led to the missing data.

In reality, data is seldom MCAR because it is such a strong assumption to make. You have to assume that the process that leads to any data being missing is independent of both the variables within your data set and other characteristics of your respondents on which you do not have any data (unobserved factors). While you can test for whether your data is MCAR (or rather, more specifically, whether your data is not MCAR) based on other variables in your data set, you cannot do the same test using data which you do not have!

You can test for whether your data is not MCAR by using the data you have which is completely observed on all your survey respondents. You do this by examining if there are statistically significant differences between respondents and non-respondents by key variables that describe your survey participants on whom you have complete information (i.e. no missing data). If there is a difference between respondents and non-respondents by any variables that characterise your sample, then you don't have a random process generating missingness, and the data is not MCAR.

It is easy to do this test for data being not MCAR when you are testing for item non-response (i.e. when your survey respondents answer some but not all of the questions). If you have item non-response, you can examine the characteristics on which you have full information from all your participants (typically their gender and age) by item non-response for particular variables which contain some amount of missingness. The steps to do this would be as follows:

1   Generate/compute a new binary variable which has the value '0' for no missingness in your variable of interest and '1' for missingness in your variable of interest.
2   Do a cross tabulation of this binary missingness variable by variables which are completely observed in your data set.
3   Use an appropriate statistical test (e.g. the chi-square test) to examine if there are significant differences between the row or column percentages.
4   Alternatively, you can do a logistic regression model with the binary missingness variable as the dependent variable and the completely observed variable as the predictor variable. You could also add in all the predictors of missingness as independent variables in the logistic regression model to find out which variables are the most important predictors of missingness (look at the size of the odds ratios).

This process of testing for whether your data is not MCAR does not work if you have unit non-response – when you have no information about the missing people who do not respond to the survey. If your data set is a longitudinal data set and you have information about who is missing in the current wave from a previous wave of data, then you could do a similar test as outlined above. However, typically as a secondary data analyst, you will not have any information about non-participants in your data. In this case, you will need to rely on the original data collectors and data depositors to provide some information about who is missing from the data. From their sampling frame, the data collectors would know who does and does not respond to their survey, and they may have some characteristics of the non-respondents, perhaps their address or age (depending on what information they have from the sampling register). The data depositors would then typically try to derive some survey weights to take account of the patterns of unit non-response from their survey. These survey weights would also normally take into account any stratification sampling methods or any **clustering** in the samples (e.g. if the sample included people living in the same household or neighbourhood).

Using these survey weights, you are making the assumption that the data is *missing at random* (MAR). This assumes that the missing patterns in your data (which are not random missing patterns) can be fully accounted for by variables where there is complete information, such as other data from the sampling frame or characteristics of the respondent on which there is complete information (no missingness). The MAR assumption cannot be verified statistically, so you as a data analyst would need to convince other people how reasonable this assumption is. You would need to analyse the patterns of missingness in your data, find out what the key predictors of those missing data are, and incorporate those predictors of missingness in your analyses. There are a number of methods that assume that the data is MAR and take account of predictors of missingness. They include survey weights that take account of the patterns of missingness, full information maximum likelihood (FIML) and multiple imputation. Before using one of these methods to compensate for missingness, you need to first carry out the four steps described above to find out what are the main predictors of missingness. And then you should add these predictors of missingness into your model of interest as survey weights, as covariates (for FIML) or as predictors of missingness in a multiple-imputation model.

Another pattern of missingness that can occur is when the reason why the data is missing for a particular variable affects the values of that variable – for example, if you are interested in measuring health through a survey but the sickest people do not respond to the survey. This pattern of missingness is called *missing not at random*. It may be that you have some predictors of health that are completely observed in the data set that also predict missing data for your incomplete health variable. You could include those predictors of health and missing health data in an analysis predicting your incomplete health variable, such as by using survey weights, FIML or multiple imputation. However, it is also possible that there are other types of predictors of missingness in your health variable that are not measured in the secondary data set but which are also correlated with health. If this is the case, one of the approaches is to do a sensitivity analysis – whereby you make assumptions on the extent to which an unobserved set of factors can predict both missingness in the dependent variable as well as the levels of your dependent variable – and see how the estimates of your model change as you increase or decrease the extent to which missing not at random is the key missing data mechanism.

Changing your research questions

One of the challenges of secondary data analysis that is not always discussed but is ever present, is the fact that you as a secondary researcher can test a range of hypotheses and select the most statistically significant associations to present your analyses in the best possible light. This often involves multiple statistical tests and multiple comparisons of results, and we know that the more statistical tests you conduct, the higher the probability that you will obtain a statistically significant p value (say less than 0.05) just by chance.

One way of reducing the chances of getting a false-positive result (type I error) is by reducing the p-value threshold to reflect the multiple statistical tests that are being made. One method is the Bonferroni correction, which divides the critical p value (α, which could be 0.05) by the number of comparisons or statistical tests being done. For example, if 10 hypotheses are being tested, the new critical p value would be $\alpha/10$ (or 0.005 if $\alpha = 0.05$). The statistical power of the study is then calculated based on this modified p value.

As a secondary data analyst, you normally will not have pre-specified hypotheses. This can result in a researcher changing their research questions and hypotheses once they get hold of the data and run some initial correlations. If you are the primary data collector, you would normally collect data to examine particular research questions, usually with some key research hypotheses or theories you wish to investigate. This constrains the primary research hypotheses of the data collector. However, a secondary data analyst is not limited to that particular set of research questions or hypotheses. Even if you pre-specify your research questions and hypotheses prior to getting the data, there is often a temptation to run more statistical tests of association and just report the most significant associations. This type of analysis is known as 'data dredging' or 'data fishing', where you don't have a priori hypotheses but instead are looking for statistically significant, but potentially meaningless, correlations. This is not science and leads to random results being reported as significant.

Data mining is the process of extracting hidden patterns from data, usually through computational algorithms. As the amount of data increases, computational methods are used to discover hidden patterns and previously undiscovered correlations. While there are similarities with data dredging, the latter usually involves some human agency (the researcher) in shaping the data mining process towards a particular set of associations. In secondary data sets, researchers have used data mining tools to look for significant predictors of missing data, rather than just relying on a priori–specified hypothetical predictors of missing data.

Another common questionable practice with secondary data is omitting data (individual records) and only selecting data that supports your own research questions. This could be analysing a subset of the sample (omitting or deleting individuals from your analysis) or reporting just a subset of all the analyses you conduct (omitting or deleting variables from your analysis). While it would be very hard to report all the analyses you conducted as a secondary data researcher, it is also your job to report all the potentially relevant sets of analyses you conducted to answer your research question.

One thing we should always remember is that non-significant results can be very interesting. This is especially true when you have strong hypotheses that are not supported by your analyses. This could possibly lead to questioning the theory that led to your hypothesis – and a new theoretical development. Unfortunately, most hypotheses in secondary research tend to be weak or confirmatory. If the hypotheses are weak, with little theoretical justification, then it will not be surprising to obtain associations that are not statistically significant. On the other hand, if the hypotheses merely confirm what existing theories and empirical analyses already show, then a significant association may not add much to the theory. So secondary researchers often have to report findings that are already known to the research community.

Showing critical awareness

There is increasing scepticism about the use of p values in reports of quantitative data analysis. The editors of the journal *The American Statistician* concluded that researchers should stop using the term *statistically significant* (Wasserstein et al., 2019). Similarly, p values should be interpreted very cautiously. 'No p-value can reveal the plausibility, presence, truth, or importance of an association or effect' (Wasserstein, Schirm & Lazar, 2019, pp. 2). Just because an association is statistically significant does not mean that an association or effect exists. Similarly, don't conclude that an association is absent just because it is statistically non-significant. We should always be sceptical about 'significant' results and studies that over-claim based solely on a p value that is less than 0.05. Instead, we should make explicit all the uncertainty that is present in any statistical test.

Many statistical analyses often do not make explicit the many assumptions underlying the statistical models. For linear regression analyses, there is a standard set of assumptions about the distribution of residuals that need to be tested. However, often such information is not presented in studies. For example, it is possible that outliers in the analyses could affect the parameters of a regression model, so it is always important to examine the data and the residuals of the model to check for potential outliers.

Another common error that some quantitative researchers make is using causal language to describe associations. For example, they may write, 'A affects B' or 'the effect of A on B', when actually what they are testing is an association (or correlation) between A and B. We all know that correlation is not the same as causation, and yet we forget about this when reporting associations.

We always need to be careful about generalising from the sample we analysed to the wider population or different populations. This is a typical mistake that occurs when researchers want to show how important their results are. However, the samples of many research data sets are not derived through a population-representative sampling process, which makes it really hard to claim that the analysis of that data set can be generalised to the wider population. Also, the context of the data collection can limit claims about generalising to other populations. For example, the historical nature of a data set or the fact that the data were collected at a particular location means that often it does not make sense to generalise from the results to other populations from different temporal or spatial locations.

Sharing your analyses and coding

It can be a bit daunting to share your analyses and statistical code (or syntax) for others to use and check. This is partly because we are afraid that others will find mistakes in our code or perhaps will not find the code so useful. However, it is really important for others to be able to reproduce your analysis. So even if other people can download the same data set from the data archive, the series of steps that occur from downloading the data set to presenting the results in a study need to be carefully documented. And a large part of this is about sharing the syntax or code that you used to derive those findings.

There are now several online repositories where researchers can upload and share syntax. If you have used data from the UKDS, then you can also upload and share your syntax. This builds a library of syntax for other users to utilise and cite. This could also enhance your reputation because it makes it easier for other researchers to use your research. The syntax created using UKDS data sets can be uploaded by clicking on 'Contribute your syntax/code' at the bottom of the respective catalogue records. Once you are logged in, the syntax files can be uploaded in various formats, including SPSS, STATA, SAS and R.

Chapter Summary

- To mitigate against the lack of appropriate data in your secondary data set, you can ask the people who deposited the data whether there are additional variables that were not deposited in the archive which you could access. You can also link in data from other data sets at an aggregate level, such as at a country, regional or district level.
- Sometimes when you don't have the specific variables you are interested in, you may be able to make do with proxy or related variables that are similar to your variable of interest.
- Limitations of secondary data analysis include the possibility that the most interesting research questions may already have been analysed and reported, you cannot collect further data on the sample (at least for that particular time and place), and your results may not match the published set of results in a report or journal article.
- The benefit of using variables already derived by the data depositors is that it gives you some reassurance that the complexity of data that goes into deriving a particular variable for analysis has already been checked and quality checked.
- It is always important to examine the reasons why some of the data is missing and explore what are some of the methods to compensate for the missingness.
- One of the challenges of secondary data analysis that is not always discussed but is ever present is the fact that you as a secondary researcher can test a range of hypotheses and select the most statistically significant associations to present your analyses in the best possible light.
- We always need to be careful about generalising from the sample we analysed to the wider population or different populations.

Further Reading

Little, R. J. A., & Rubin, D. B. (2002). *Statistical analysis with missing data: Little/ statistical analysis with missing data*. Wiley.

9

CONCLUSIONS

TARANI CHANDOLA

Chapter Overview

Next steps in secondary data analysis 132

Critics of secondary analysis 133

The future of secondary data 134

Further Reading 136

Next steps in secondary data analysis

You as the secondary data researcher are essentially analysing data which you have not been involved in the process of collecting. You are 'at a distance' from the data. On the one hand, this could be quite a good thing, because you are 'more objective'. You are a 'dispassionate observer' of associations in the data, rather than someone who has collected the data for a particular purpose and with a possible interest in demonstrating an association. However, this could also be a bad thing, as you are not immersed in the data process, and the meanings and contexts of the data and data collection process are unknown to you, except what you learn through the data documentation. Some people have interpreted this as part of the quantitative/qualitative divide, asserting that qualitative researchers are grounded in the data they collect, in contrast to the large and largely secondary data sets that many quantitative researchers analyse. Some of these criticisms are now no longer valid as qualitative data has now been deposited in archives for secondary data analysis. Hence, there is no longer a strict qualitative/quantitative divide in secondary data analysis. Moreover, this criticism assumes that the only type of valid data for social researchers is data that the researchers directly collect themselves. As a result, large-scale data collections on hundreds and thousands of people are deemed to be not so interesting as a single researcher is unlikely to collect such vast amounts of data by themselves. This criticism can be turned on its head, as secondary data is often collected by large teams of researchers and data collectors, enabling large numbers of people to be researched. Furthermore, there are many large-scale data collection activities where both qualitative and quantitative data are collected for analysis – such as intervention studies, which study whether particular interventions work and, if so, how they work and what are the processes that lead to such interventions working or not working. However, it is still rare for such combinations of qualitative and quantitative secondary data sets to be deposited in data archives.

The use of secondary data is common in some social science disciplines such as economics, although in other disciplines such as sociology, secondary analysis was not a popular approach and was presumed to be inferior to primary data collection and analysis. This was partly because it was deemed to be less original, with less potential for discovering new social facts leading to new theories. Secondary data analysis was perceived to be merely confirming existing hypotheses, partly because the data was often collected around specific hypotheses and research questions, which were then answered by the original primary data researchers. However, this criticism assumes that all the interesting research questions have already been answered by the original data collectors and researchers. This is an unrealistic assumption as there is a wealth of data that is collected for secondary analyses, often without any specific research questions or hypotheses in mind. This leaves a substantial 'open door' for secondary researchers to discover new social facts that could lead to modifying or discovering new social theories.

Critics of secondary analysis

Ethical risks and informed consent, confidentiality and anonymity

It is essential that secondary data is protected and processed in an ethical manner and in compliance with all the laws and regulations that apply to such data, such as the EU General Data Protection Regulation. Just because you have access to the data does not mean that you can ethically or legally reuse the data for your intended analysis, purpose or research.

Ethical concerns around secondary data analysis tend to be less prevalent than in primary data collection. Secondary data that is deposited in data archives has already been through an ethical review process. Primary data collectors need to demonstrate that they have obtained relevant and informed consent from their participants not only to collect and analyse the data but also to share their data more widely with the research community. They also need to show that they have reduced the chances of identifying any specific individuals from their data. The data archives would also process the data before release, using software and other tools to reduce the chances that any individual person from the data set can be identified. This is often done by eliminating some identifying variables from the data set, such as the location of the sample participant, and also by making some detailed categories of variables broader, such as transforming the specific date of birth into just the year of birth.

Secondary data can vary in terms of the amount of identifying information in it. If the data has no information that can identify individuals and they are anonymised, then it is very unlikely that a secondary data analysis will require a review by an ethical research board. However, if there is some possibility that individuals can be identified, then there usually is some review of the research proposed by a secondary data analyst. If the data is obtained from a data archive, and either identifying or sensitive data is requested by the secondary data analyst, then it is common for the data archive to request additional information from the researcher, such as their research plans and additional confirmation that they will treat the data securely and will not release any data that could identify individuals. For some secondary data, there will be additional guarantees sought by the data archive or data depositor, such as details on your computing and data environment, and how secure your data processing environment is. Here, it is likely that you will need the help of the information governance or data protection team at your university or institution to help convince the data archive that your research environment is secure.

If the secondary data is freely available on the internet, in books or in other public forums, permission for further use and analysis is implied. Data of this type is often covered by an 'open data licence'. You should always check what the data can be used for, and permission should be gained from the data owner for any reuse not covered by a licence. In all cases, the original source should be referenced. This is also true for secondary data sets in data archives – the original data depositors should be acknowledged and the data referenced appropriately with the DOI (if available) or a hyperlink to the original online data source.

The key ethical concern for secondary data researchers is that they need to keep their data secure and destroy the data sets after having completed their research. This means making sure the data is kept safe from unauthorized access, such as by keeping it in a password-protected or encrypted file. Data in the form of hard copies should be kept in safe, locked cabinets, whereas soft copies should be kept as encrypted files in computers. Data should not be kept on cloud storage locations unless this is permitted by the data depositors. Furthermore, the secondary researcher needs to prevent accidental loss of data, such as losing data stored on pen drives or laptops. Having any data on mobile computing devices encrypted is one of the ways of reducing the risk of losing data.

Data should not be stored for a longer period than is necessary for research purposes. This means that after you have finished analysing your research questions and published your results, you are expected to delete the data from your computers, data storage devices and locations.

The future of secondary data

Funding agencies like the UK ESRC invest considerable amounts of funding in secondary data analysis, whether through providing funding for data infrastructure projects like the UKDS or for their Secondary Data Analysis Initiative (https://esrc.ukri.org/research/our-research/secondary-data-analysis-initiative). They acknowledge that the UK is a world leader in data infrastructure for social and economic research, which provides a huge opportunity to address some of the most pressing challenges facing society today and in the future. The secondary data initiative from the ESRC aims to deliver high-quality, high-impact research through a deeper exploitation of major data resources created by the ESRC and other agencies.

Alongside the use of resources from data archives, the use of administrative data for research purposes is also becoming more common in the UK and elsewhere. The use of administrative data sets in research is common in some European countries (most notably the Nordic countries). Such administrative data are also secondary data sets, although they tend not to be found in data archives. Researchers also link the administrative data records of participants in their own studies to their data. For example, Understanding Society and the MCS have linked administrative educational data (from the National Pupil Database) to their studies. Other studies have linked or plan to link to health records and employment and pension records. Access to these administrative data sets is often less straightforward than access to secondary data from data archives. This is mostly due to the high risk of identifying individuals and the amount of sensitive and personal data contained in administrative data sets. There are increasing amounts of funding available, at least from UK funding agencies, to use such data for research purposes.

With the increase in funding for secondary data analysis, in the amounts of secondary and administrative data available for research and in the number of qualified researchers to analyse such data, it is likely that secondary data analysis will continue to be a key research mode in the social sciences.

Chapter Summary

- As a secondary researcher, you are 'at a distance' from the data. On the one hand, this could be quite a good thing, because you are 'more objective'. However, this could also be a bad thing, as you are not immersed in the data process, and the meanings and contexts of the data and data collection process are unknown to you. Some people have interpreted this as part of the quantitative/qualitative divide; however, these criticisms are now no longer valid as qualitative data have now been deposited in archives for secondary data analysis.
- It is essential that secondary data is protected and processed in an ethical manner and in compliance with all the laws and regulations that apply to such data, such as the EU General Data Protection Regulation.
- Ethical concerns around secondary data analysis tend to be less prominent than in primary data collection.
- If the secondary data is freely available on the internet, in books or in other public forums, permission for further use and analysis is implied.
- The key ethical concern for secondary data researchers is that they need to keep their data secure and destroy the data sets after having completed their research. Data should not be stored for a longer period than is necessary for research purposes.
- Funding agencies like the UK ESRC invest considerable amounts of funding in secondary data analysis, and it is likely that secondary data analysis will continue to be a key research mode for the social sciences.

Further Reading

Tripathy, J. P. (2013). Secondary data analysis: Ethical issues and challenges. *Iranian Journal of Public Health, 42*(12), 1478–1479.

APPENDIX 1

CASE STUDY EXAMPLE OF SECONDARY DATA ANALYSIS USING BIOMARKER DATA FROM UNDERSTANDING SOCIETY, THE UK HOUSEHOLD LONGITUDINAL STUDY

CARA BOOKER

Introduction

In this appendix, we will be showing you an example of data analysis that uses bio-marker data from the UK Household Longitudinal Study (UKHLS). Biomarkers are measureable markers of biological conditions or states. Biomarkers include non-blood-based markers, such as height, weight, blood pressure, lung function and grip strength, and blood-based markers, such as HbA1c (glycated hemoglobin), c-reactive protein (CRP), testosterone, cortisol and fibrinogen, to name just a few. In waves 2 and 3, UKHLS conducted nurse surveys and collected biomarkers from consenting participants (www.understandingsociety.ac.uk/documentation/health-assessment). We will be using this data to try and answer the following question:

> Who is more stressed at work? Is it those at the top of the social position ladder or those at the bottom?

This is the same question that was asked in Chapter 6; however, instead of using job stress, we will be using inflammatory and hormone biomarkers as proxies for stress.

Conceptualising and measuring the independent variable

In Chapter 6, we used highest educational qualifications; however, there are other measures of socio-economic position (SEP), including social class, income, wealth, and measures of poverty or deprivation, to name just a few. Each of these may 'measure' something slightly different; for example, social class may be a measure of occupational prestige, while educational attainment may be a measure of resources or economic potential. UKHLS collects many of these markers of SEP, and for these analyses, we will be using two: highest educational qualifications and social class.

We will not describe highest educational qualifications, as it is described in Chapter 6; however, the measure of social class we are going to use is the National Statistics Socio-Economic Classification (NS-SEC). The NS-SEC is a UK measure of employment 'relations and conditions of occupations' (www.ons.gov.uk/methodology/classifications andstandards/otherclassifications/thenationalstatisticssocioeconomicclassificationnssecrebasedonsoc2010). The NS-SEC can be coded into an eight-, five-, or three-category variable. We will be using the NS-SEC five-category variable. The five categories are as follows:

1   Higher managerial, administrative and professional occupations
2   Intermediate occupations
3   Small employers and own-account workers
4   Lower supervisory and technical occupations
5   Semi-routine and routine occupations

Note that there is no category in the five-category measure for individuals who have never worked or have been long-term unemployed. The eight-category measure does include a category for these individuals.

Conceptualising and measuring the dependent variables

The dependent variables we are going to be looking at for this example are six biomarkers: CRP, cytomegalovirus (CMV) immunoglobulin (Ig) M and CMV IgG, insulin-like growth factor-1 (IGF-1), testosterone and dihydroepiandrosterone sulphate (DHEAS).

All information provided on the biomarkers can be found in the UKHLS *Biomarker User Guide and Glossary* (www.understandingsociety.ac.uk/sites/default/files/down loads/documentation/health/user-guides/7251-UnderstandingSociety-Biomarker-UserGuide-2014.pdf).

CRP is a protein in the blood that increases when inflammation occurs and is part of the body's defence mechanism. CRP levels greater than 3 mg/L are considered a risk factor for cardiovascular disease and indicate systemic inflammation. CRP also increases due to recent infection, which is indicated by levels greater than 10 mg/L. Therefore, it is recommended that individuals with these levels of CRP be deleted from the analysis as they may bias the findings. Additionally, CRP levels can be influenced by different types of medication, such as anti-inflammatories, statins and contraception and hormone replacement therapy; therefore, it is preferred that we include use of these medications in our analyses to control for any influence they may have on CRP levels. CRP is a continuous variable.

CMV IgM and CMV IgG are antibodies in the blood that indicate the workings of an individual's immune system. CMV is a herpes virus that can stay in the body without producing any symptoms. The two antibodies indicate different temporal reactions to infections: IgG indicates that at some point in time the individual had a CMV infection, while IgM indicates a recent infection. Levels of IgM and IgG decrease with illness and age. As these two measures indicate whether an individual has had an infection, the variables are categorical, with three categories: 1 = *antibody detected*, 2 = *antibody not detected* and 3 = *indeterminate*.

IGF-1 is a hormone that has been shown to be associated with heart disease at low levels and some cancers at high levels. It is important for growth and development in childhood and continues to be important in building up organs and tissues into adulthood. IGF-1 is a continuous variable, and levels may differ between men and women and by age.

Testosterone is an anabolic steroid and, similar to IGF-1, is involved in building up tissues as well as muscles. It is most commonly known for playing an integral role in the development of male secondary sexual characteristics. Testosterone is a continuous variable and varies during the day, with higher values in the morning. Thus, one may want to consider the time of day the sample was collected when analysing.

DHEAS is a steroid hormone, the most common in the body. DHEAS has been associated with cardiovascular health, and levels decline with age. DHEAS is a continuous variable.

Control variables

In this example, we are using the following control variables: age, gender for all models and anti-inflammatories, statins and contraception and hormone replacement therapy for the CRP models.

Age is a continuous variable. Gender, anti-inflammatories, statins and contraception and hormone replacement therapy are binary variables.

Data management

Step 1: Downloading the biomarker data set

The biomarker data sets can be downloaded from the UK Data Service. As the nurse visits occurred across two waves, waves 2 and 3, there are wave-specific data sets. However, there are also data sets that combine the two waves together; these are the data sets we will be using. The two data sets you will be using are xindresp_ns and xlabblood_ns. The xindresp_ns data set contains variables from the nurse survey, including medication and anthropometric biomarkers such as grip strength, waist circumference and weight. The nurse survey data set also contains selected variables, including derived variables, from the corresponding wave of data collection. The xlabblood_ns contains the blood biomarker data.

Step 2: Merging nurse visit data with biomarker data

To merge the data, use the following STATA code:

```
use "file location\xindresp_ns", clear
merge m:1 pidp using "file location\xlabblood_ns"
drop _merge
```

Here, we use the type statement 1:1 in the merge command to tell STATA to merge one record from the xindresp_ns data set with one record from the xlabblood_ns data set, matching on the key variable pidp.

Step 3: Selecting our sample and keeping selected variables

As in the example in Chapter 6, we are only including individuals who are currently working and dropping all other individuals.

*Keeping respondents who are in work

keep if jbstat == 2

The nurse data set, xindresp_ns, contains more than 350 variables, and we will not need to use most of them, so we will select the ones we want to keep.

*Keeping susbset of variables

keep pid wave nsex age omsysval omdiaval ompulval wstval sf1 health marstat hiqual_dv scghq1_dv jbnssec5_dv bmival urban_dv psu strata bnf7_conhrt bnf7_antifibs bnf7_aspirin bnf7_statins bnf7_antiinflam bnf7_antiep indnsub_lw indnsub_xw dheas cmvavc uscmm uscmg testo igfi hscrp

Rather that set missing indicators to 'missing' at each step, we will do it in one step here.

*Recoding missing indicators

recode omsysval omdiaval ompulval wstval sf1 health marstat hiqual_dv scghq1_dv jbnssec5_dv bmival urban_dv psu strata bnf7_conhrt bnf7_antifibs bnf7_aspirin bnf7_statins bnf7_antiinflam bnf7_antiep dord dory dorm dheas cmvavc uscmm uscmg testo igfi hscrp (-41/-1=.)

Step 4: Transformation of dependent variables

As noted in the earlier section on dependent variables, CRP values greater than 10 should be deleted.

*Set CRP values over 10 to 'missing'

recode hscrp 10/max=.

We also want to test for normality of our variables and if they are non-normally distributed and then transform them to make them more normal:

*Test for normality of continuous dependent variables

summ dheas testo igfi hscrp,d

Our results show us that all of these biomarkers are skewed and non-normally distributed, thus we will use log transformation to create variables that are more normally distributed.

```
*Normalizing selected variables – log transformation
local varlista "dheas testo igfi hscrp"
foreach var in `varlista' {
    gen log`var'=log10(`var')
}
```

Step 5: Transformation of independent variables

We will combine other qualifications with no qualifications in the highest educational qualifications variable.

```
gen hiqual_dv5 = hiqual_dv
*Recode b_hiqual_dv5: recode no qualification (9) to same category as other
qualification (5)
recode hiqual_dv5 9=5
*Label newly created variable
label var hiqual_dv5 "Five Category Educational Qualifications"
*Label variable categories
label define hql   1 "Degree" ///
                   2 "Other higher" ///
                   3 "A level" ///
                   4 "GCSE" ///
                   5 "No/other qualification"


label define nss   1 "Management & Professional" ///
                   2 "Intermediate" ///
                   3 "Small employers & own account" ///
                   4 "Lower supervisory & technical" ///
                   5 "Semi-routine & routine"
```

*Assign category labels to associated variables

label values hiqual_dv5 hql

label values jbnssec5_dv nss

Univariate distributions

To examine the univariate distributions of the independent and dependent variables, we use both graphs and tables. First, we will start with the independent variables.

*Histograms for independent variables

*Education

hist hiqual_dv5, freq

The resulting graph is seen in Figure A1.1.

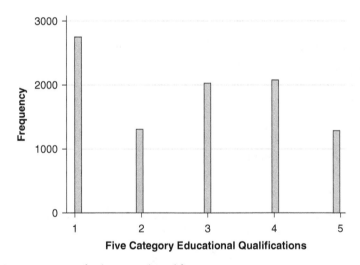

Figure A1.1   Histogram of educational qualifications

As you can see, category 1, Degree, has a higher frequency than all the other categories, while categories 2 and 5, Other higher and No/other qualifications, respectively, have the lowest.

Now we will look at the social class distribution (Figure A1.2).

*Social class

hist jbnssec5_dv, freq

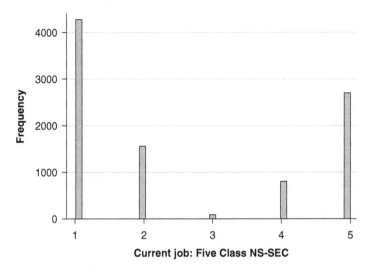

Figure A1.2 Histogram of social class

Note. NS-SEC = National Statistics Socio-Economic Classification.

Here, we see that category 3, Small Employers & Own Account, has the lowest frequency; this is due to our dropping all own-account individuals from our sample. Category 1, Management & Professional, is the largest category.

Next we will look at the dependent variables. As we have both categorical and continuous variables, we will need to separate them. We will first look at the distributions of the categorical variables.

*Table for categorical biomarkers – IgM & IgG

tab1 uscmm uscmg

Using the information provided from this command, we will create a table with the relevant information (Table A1.1).

Table A1.1 Frequencies of IgM and IgG

	IgM		IgG	
Category	**N**	**%**	**N**	**%**
Detected	105	2	2606	43
Not detected	5910	97	3465	57
Indeterminate	94	2	38	1

Note. Ig = immunoglobulin.

Here, we see that the majority of individuals (97%) have non-detectable IgM – meaning that they have not had a recent CMV infection. A smaller percentage (57%) of individuals have a non-detectable IgG level, while 43% have a detectable level – meaning that at some point in their lives these individuals had a CMV infection.

Next, we will have to examine the mean scores for the continuous dependent variables.

*Means of continuous biomarkers

summ logdheas logtesto logigfi loghscrp

The output from this command is seen in Table A1.2.

Table A1.2   Means of continuous biomarkers

Variable	Obs	Mean	Std. Dev.	Min	Max
logdheas	6,105	1.499614	.6741581	-2.302585	3.230804
logtesto	3,860	2.006427	1.115571	-2.302585	3.7281
logigfi	6,079	2.900776	.3358966	1.098612	4.356709
loghscrp	5,660	.2167503	.9378499	-1.609438	2.292535

Here, we see that there are differences in observation numbers across the biomarkers. We are also given the means and standard deviations for each one. Remember that these are logged values, which is why we have minimum values that are negative.

Bivariate distributions

The next step in analysing data is to examine the bivariate relationships between our dependent and independent variables. In this case, we have two independent variables and six dependent variables, resulting in 12 bivariate tables or graphs. We start with categorical biomarker by bivariate distributions.

Using tab2 tells STATA to cross-tab the two variables listed, and chi2 provides test statistics for the chi-square test (Tables A1.3 and A1.4).

*Cross tabulation of IgM by Educational qualifications

tab2 uscmm hiqual_dv5, column chi2

*Cross tabulation of IgG by Educational qualifications

tab2 uscmg hiqual_dv5, column chi2

Table A1.3 Frequencies of IgM by educational qualifications

Key	
frequency *column percentage*	

cytomegalo virus (cmv) igm	Five Category Educational Qualifications					Total
	1	2	3	4	5	
1	27 1.56	15 1.72	22 1.69	18 1.32	23 2.81	105 1.73
2	1,670 96.76	842 96.78	1,264 97.16	1,330 97.44	778 94.99	5,884 96.76
3	29 1.68	13 1.49	15 1.15	17 1.25	18 2.20	92 1.51
Total	1,726 100.00	870 100.00	1,301 100.00	1,365 100.00	819 100.00	6,081 100.00

Pearson chi2(8) = 12.1080   Pr = 0.146

Table A1.4 Frequencies of IgG by educational qualifications

Key	
frequency *column percentage*	

cytomegalo virus (cmv) igg	Five Category Educational Qualifications					Total
	1	2	3	4	5	
1	687 39.80	360 41.38	517 39.74	601 44.03	429 52.38	2,594 42.66
2	1,027 59.50	505 58.05	778 59.80	757 55.46	382 46.64	3,449 56.72
3	12 0.70	5 0.57	6 0.46	7 0.51	8 0.98	38 0.62
Total	1,726 100.00	870 100.00	1,301 100.00	1,365 100.00	819 100.00	6,081 100.00

Pearson chi2(8) = 47.4595   Pr = 0.000

From the results in Table A1.3, we can see that the distribution of detectable IgM is slightly higher in the No/other category (5); however, when you look at the Pearson chi-square test at the bottom, you see that the *p* value is large and thus the distributions across the categories are not different from each other.

Unlike Table A1.3, in Table A1.4, the distribution of detectable IgG varies more across the educational qualification groups, and the statistics at the bottom of the table indicate that these distributions are different from each other.

We then repeat this step for the social class variables (Tables A1.5 and A1.6).

*Cross tabulation of IgM by social class

tab2 uscmm jbnssec5, column chi2

Table A1.5 Frequencies of IgM by social class

Key
frequency
column percentage

cytomegalo virus (cmv) igm	Current job: Five Class NS-SEC					
	1	2	3	4	5	Total
1	45	17	3	9	31	105
	1.64	1.73	4.55	1.62	1.83	1.74
2	2,662	955	63	540	1,634	5,854
	96.84	97.05	95.45	97.12	96.34	96.74
3	42	12	0	7	31	92
	1.53	1.22	0.00	1.26	1.83	1.52
Total	2,749	984	66	556	1,696	6,051
	100.00	100.00	100.00	100.00	100.00	100.00

Pearson chi2(8) = 6.2386   Pr = 0.621

There is a similar finding in Table A1.5 as in the educational qualifications table (Table A1.3), with no differences in the distribution across the social class groups by IgM categories.

*Cross tabulation of IgG by social class

tab2 uscmg jbnssec5, column chi2

In Table A1.6, we observe that the percentage of detectable IgG varies across the social class groups (similar to the pattern for educational qualifications in Table A1.4).

Table A1.6 Frequencies of IgG by social class

Key
frequency
column percentage

cytomegalo virus (cmv) igg	Current job: Five Class NS-SEC					Total
	1	2	3	4	5	
1	1,110	407	24	230	811	2,582
	40.38	41.36	36.36	41.37	47.82	42.67
2	1,622	570	42	322	875	3,431
	59.00	57.93	63.64	57.91	51.59	56.70
3	17	7	0	4	10	38
	0.62	0.71	0.00	0.72	0.59	0.63
Total	2,749	984	66	556	1,696	6,051
	100.00	100.00	100.00	100.00	100.00	100.00

Pearson chi2(8) = 27.1329   Pr = 0.001

In both the IgM and the IgG table, we observe very small numbers of people in the intermediate category (3). In fact, there are no individuals in the small employers and own-account category (3), so we will set these to 'missing' for the remainder of the analyses.

*Setting indeterminate to missing for IgM and IgG

recode uscmm 3=.

recode uscmg 3=.

Now that these are binary variables, we will recode to 0/1 so that *not detected* = 0 and *detected* = 1.

recode uscmm 2=0

recode uscmg 2=0

The next bivariate associations we will look at are the means of the four continuous biomarkers across the different educational or social class groups, starting with educational qualifications.

oneway logdheas hiqual_dv5, tabulate

oneway logtesto hiqual_dv5, tabulate

oneway logigfi hiqual_dv5, tabulate

oneway loghscrp hiqual_dv5, tabulate

Taking the information provided from the output, we create a table (Table A1.7).

Table A1.7 Means of biomarkers by educational qualification

| | Educational Qualification, Mean (SD) | | | | | |
Biomarker	Degree	Other Higher Qualifications	A Level	GCSE	No/Other Qualifications	p Value
DHEAS	1.55 (0.64)	1.47 (0.65)	1.58 (0.67)	1.51 (0.68)	1.27 (0.73)	0.0000
Testosterone	1.98 (1.14)	1.90 (1.15)	2.11 (1.07)	1.94 (1.13)	2.13 (1.04	0.0003
IGF-1	2.96 (0.31)	2.87 (0.33)	2.93 (0.34)	2.90 (0.35)	2.77 (0.33)	0.0000
CRP	0.04 (0.94)	0.27 (0.94)	0.22 (0.95)	0.26 (0.92)	0.46 (0.88)	0.0000

Note. GCSE = General Certificate of Secondary Education; DHEAS = dihydroepiandrosterone sulphate; IGF-1 = insulin-like growth factor-1; CRP = c-reactive protein.

We can see that there are differences in means between educational qualification groups. For example, individuals in the No/other qualifications group have the lowest levels of DHEAS compared with all other groups. Conversely, this group has the highest levels of CRP relative to the other groups, indicating that individuals in this group may have systemic inflammation whereas individuals in the Degree category (1) do not.

Here is the same code but for social class:

oneway logdheas jbnssec5_dv, tabulate

oneway logtesto jbnssec5_dv, tabulate

oneway logigfi jbnssec5_dv, tabulate

oneway loghscrp jbnssec5_dv, tabulate

The resulting table is Table A1.8.

Table A1.8 Means of biomarkers by social class

| | Social Class, Mean (SD) | | | | | |
Biomarker	Management and Professional	Intermediate	Small Employers and Own Account	Lower Supervisory and Technical	Semi-Routine and Routine	p Value
DHEAS	1.52 (0.64)	1.43 (0.67)	1.45 (0.57)	1.65 (0.62)	1.45 (0.73)	0.0000
Testosterone	2.02 (1.10)	1.73 (1.18)	2.35 (0.88)	2.43 (0.87)	1.92 (1.17)	0.0000
IGF-1	2.91 (0.31)	2.90 (0.34)	2.78 (0.30)	2.91 (0.35)	2.88 (0.36)	0.0059
CRP	0.15 (0.93)	0.21 (0.95)	0.02 (0.93)	0.22 (0.92)	0.34 (0.94)	0.0000

Note. DHEAS = dihydroepiandrosterone sulphate; IGF-1 = insulin-like growth factor-1; CRP = c-reactive protein.

Individuals who are in the lower supervisory and technical social class have the highest levels of DHEAS and testosterone. Individuals in semi-routine and routine occupations have the highest levels of CRP compared with the other groups. Looking across the groups, there does not appear to be any discernible pattern; that is, levels do not increase or decrease in a specific manner across the groups.

Multivariate analysis

Now that we have examined the bivariate relationships, we will examine the multivariate relationships by conducting linear and logistic regression and including covariates in the models.

Step 1: Describing the dependent variables

Here, we will describe the dependent variables by one of our covariates, gender, and test for differences in distributions and means using chi-square and independent *t* test, respectively.

*Frequencies of categorical variables by gender

tab2 nsex (uscmm uscmg), column row chi2

*Means of continuous variables by gender

ttest logdheas, by(nsex)

ttest logtesto, by(nsex)

ttest logigfi, by(nsex)

ttest loghscrp, by(nsex)

We then create a descriptive table (Table A1.9) using the resultant output.

Table A1.9 Descriptive statistics of biomarkers by gender

Biomarker	Overall (%) I	Gender (%) Men	Women	p Value
CMV IgM				
Detected	2	1	2	
Not detected	98	99	98	0.08
CMV IgG				
Detected	43	40	46	
Not detected	57	60	54	0.0000

	Overall (%)	Gender (%)		
	Mean (*SD*)	Mean (*SD*)	Mean (*SD*)	
DHEAS	1.78 (0.57)	1.50 (0.67)	1.27 (0.66)	0.0000
Testosterone	2.01 (1.12)	2.66 (0.39)	0.37 (0.47)	0.0000
IGF-1	2.90 (0.34	2.92 (0.31)	2.88 (0.36)	0.0000
CRP	0.22 (0.94)	0.14 (0.90)	0.28 (0.96)	0.0000

Note. Logged DHEAS, testosterone, IGF-1 and CRP values. Ig = immunoglobulin; CMV = cytomegalovirus; DHEAS = dihydroepiandrosterone sulphate; IGF-1 = insulin-like growth factor-1; CRP = c-reactive protein.

The accompanying text in a report or paper would be as follows:

Only 2% of individuals had detectable IgM levels in their blood, and this did not differ between men and women. A larger percentage (43%) had detectable IgG levels, but unlike for IgM, there were gender differences. A larger percentage of women (46%) had detectable levels of IgG compared with men (40%). Men had higher levels of DHEAS, mean = 1.60, *SD* = 0.67, compared with women, mean = 1.27, *SD* = 0.66. As would be expected, men had vastly higher levels of testosterone, mean = 2.66, *SD* = 0.39, compared with women, mean = 0.37, *SD* = 0.47. Men also had higher levels of IGF-1, mean = 2.92, *SD* = 0.31, than women, mean = 2.88, *SD* = 0.36. CRP was the only biomarker where women had higher levels, mean = 0.28, *SD* = 0.96, than men, mean = 0.14, *SD* = 0.90.

Step 2: Regression analyses

Now we turn to regression analyses to further examine the relationship between the biomarkers and measures of socio-economic position. We will include covariates in these models as described in the section on control variables: age, gender and medication use (in the CRP model only). This time we will use the same svy commands that we used in Chapter 6.

*Survey set the data

svyset psu [pweight= indnsub_lw], strata(strata) singleunit(scaled)

First, we will run models with educational qualifications as the independent variable. We start with the linear models for the continuous biomarkers.

*Linear regression models for continuous biomarkers

xi: svy: regress logdheas ib1.hiqual_dv5 i.nsex age

xi: svy: regress logtesto ib1.hiqual_dv5 i.nsex age

xi: svy: regress logigfi ib1.hiqual_dv5 i.nsex age

xi: svy: regress loghscrp i.hiqual_dv5 i.nsex age bnf7_conhrt bnf7_statins bnf7_antiinflam

The output can be seen in Table A1.10.

Table A1.10 Linear regression estimates of selected biomarkers on highest educational qualifications

Highest Educational Qualification	DHEAS, β (95% CI)	Testosterone, β (95% CI)	IGF-1, β (95% CI)	CRP, β (95% CI)
Degree (reference)				
Other higher qualifications	0.02 [−0.03, 0.07]	0.02 [−0.03, 0.07]	−0.05 [−0.08, 0.02]	0.25 [0.10, 0.40]
A level, etc.	−0.005 [−0.05, 0.04]	0.02 [−0.02, 0.06]	0.02 [−0.04, 0.008]	0.18 [0.03, 0.33]
GCSE, etc.	0.04 [−0.009, 0.08]	0.02 [−0.02, 0.07]	−0.03 [−0.06, −0.005]	0.23 [0.09, 0.37]
No/other qualifications	−0.01 [−0.07, 0.05]	0.03 [−0.03, 0.09]	−0.05 [−0.08, −0.02]	0.34 [0.20, 0.49]

Note. DHEAS, IGF-1 and testosterone models were controlled for age and gender; CRP model was controlled for age, gender and contraceptive hormones. DHEAS = dihydroepiandrosterone sulphate; IGF-1 = insulin-like growth factor-1; CRP = c-reactive protein; CI = confidence interval; GCSE = General Certificate of Secondary Education.

This is an example of how you might write up this table:

Levels of DHEAS or testosterone did not differ between educational groups after controlling for age and gender. However, there were some differences in IGF-1 and CRP levels. Individuals who had GCSE qualifications had IGF-1 levels that were 3% lower than those of individuals with a degree, $\beta = -0.03$, 95% confidence interval (CI) = [−0.06, −0.005]. Similarly, individuals with no or other qualifications had 5% lower levels of IGF-1, $\beta = -0.05$, 95% CI = [−0.08, −0.02]. Compared with individuals with a degree, individuals in all other educational qualification groups had higher levels of CRP. Most notably, individuals with no or other qualifications had 34% higher levels of CRP, $\beta = 0.34$, 95% CI = [0.20, 0.49], than individuals with a degree.

Next, we run logistic regression models for IgM and IgG. As these are binary variables, we will ask for odds ratios (ORs) to be provided rather than regression coefficients.

*Logistic regressions for ordinal biomarkers

xi: svy: logit uscmm ib1.hiqual_dv5 i.nsex age, or

xi: svy: logit uscmg ib1.hiqual_dv5 i.nsex age, or

In Table A1.11, we observe the following. Detectable levels of IgM did not differ across the educational qualification groups compared with the Degree group. The odds of having detectable levels of IgG were higher in the lowest educational qualification group, No/other qualifications, $OR = 1.29$, 95% CI = [1.02, 1.64], compared with the odds for individuals with a degree.

Table A1.11 Logistic regression odds ratios of IgM and IgG on highest educational qualifications

Highest Educational Qualification	CMV IgM		CMV IgG	
	Not Detected (Reference)	Detected, *OR* (95% CI)	Not Detected (Reference)	Detected, *OR* (95% CI)
Degree (reference)				
Other higher qualifications		1.27 [0.62, 2.58]		0.94 [0.76, 1.15]
A level, etc.		1.14 [0.56, 2.33]		0.98 [0.81, 1.18]
GCSE, etc.		0.74 [0.36, 1.53]		1.07 [0.89, 1.27]
No/other qualifications		1.78 [0.90, 3.52]		1.29 [1.02, 1.64]

Note. Models were controlled for age and gender. All models were weighted for selection probability and blood measures non-response. CMV = cytomegalovirus; Ig = immunoglobulin; *OR* = odds ratio; CI = confidence interval; GCSE = General Certificate of Secondary Education.

We repeat these analyses for the social class independent variable.

*Linear regression for continuous biomarkers

xi: svy: regress logdheas ib1.jbnssec5_dv i.nsex age

xi: svy: regress logtesto ib1.jbnssec5_dv i.nsex age

xi: svy: regress logigfi ib1.jbnssec5_dv i.nsex age

xi: svy: regress loghscrp i.jbnssec5_dv i.nsex age bnf7_conhrt bnf7_statins bnf7_antiinflam

The results from these regressions (Table A1.12) differ from those observed for educational qualifications. Again, there are no differences in the levels of DHEAS or IGF-1 between the lower social class groups and the Management & professional group. Individuals in the Semi-routine and routine social class had 6% higher levels of testosterone than individuals in the Management & professional social class, β = .06, 95% CI = [0.02, 0.10]. This was also true for CRP, where those in semi-routine and routine occupations had 18% higher levels than individuals in management or professional occupations, β = .18, 95% CI = [0.07, 0.29].

Finally, we run the logistic models for IgM and IgG.

* Logistic regressions for ordinal biomarkers

xi: svy: logit uscmm ib1.jbnssec5_dv i.nsex age, or

xi: svy: logit uscmg ib1.jbnssec5_dv i.nsex age, or

Again, in Table A1.13, we do not observe differences between the lower social class groups and the Management & professional group for IgM. Similar to the findings

Table A1.12 Linear regression estimates of selected biomarkers on social class

Social Class	DHEAS, β (95% CI)	Testosterone, β (95% CI)	IGF-1, β (95% CI)	CRP, β (95% CI)
Management and professional (reference)				
Intermediate	−0.004 [−0.05, 0.04]	−0.005 [−0.05, 0.04]	−0.002 [−0.03, 0.02]	0.02 [−0.11, 0.15]
Small employers and own account	0.08 [−0.07, 0.23]	0.0003 [−0.16, 0.16]	−0.05 [−0.14, 0.03]	−0.002 [−0.39, 0.39]
Lower supervisory and own account	0.01 [−0.05, 0.08]	0.06 [−0.003, 0.12]	−0.005 [−0.04, 0.03]	0.07 [−0.11, 0.26]
Semi-routine and routine	0.01 [−0.03, 0.05]	0.06 [0.02, 0.10]	0.01 [−0.03, 0.01]	0.18 [0.07, 0.29]

Note. DHEAS = dihydroepiandrosterone sulphate; IGF = insulin-like growth factor; CRP = c-reactive protein; CI = confidence interval.

from Table A1.12, only individuals in semi-routine and routine occupations had increased odds of having detectable IgG compared with individuals in management and professional occupations, *OR* = 1.40, 95% CI = [1.20, 1.63].

Table A1.13 Logistic regression odds ratios of IgM and IgG and social class

Social Class	CMV IgM Not Detected (Reference)	CMV IgM Detected, OR (95% CI)	CMV IgG Not Detected (Reference)	CMV IgG Detected, OR (95% CI)
Management and professional (reference)				
Intermediate		1.08 [0.54, 2.16]		1.02 [0.84, 1.25]
Small employers and own account		3.35 [0.92, 12.20]		0.75 [0.35, 1.59]
Lower supervisory and own account		0.84 [0.30, 2.41]		1.19 [0.94, 1.51]
Semi-routine and routine		1.11 [0.64, 1.93]		1.40 [1.20, 1.63]

Note. Models were controlled for age and gender. All models were weighted for selection probability and blood measures non-response. CMV = cytomegalovirus; Ig = immunoglobulin; OR = odds ratio; CI = confidence interval.

Conclusion

Now that we have concluded our analyses, what does all of this mean? What is the answer to our original research question: Who is more stressed at work? Is it those at the top of the social position ladder or those at the bottom?

In general, we did not find many differences in the levels of either inflammatory or hormone biomarkers once we controlled for age and gender. In the bivariate associations, we observed differences for all biomarkers except IgM for both educational qualifications and social class. However, once we ran multivariate analyses and controlled for age and gender, most of these differences disappeared. For the differences that remained, we did observe that the lowest groups, in either education or social class, had lower levels of biomarkers, IGF-1, CRP and IgG in the case of educational qualifications and CRP and IgG for social class.

One of the contrasts between educational qualifications and social class can be observed in CRP. All educational qualification groups had increased levels of CRP compared with the Degree group; however, it was only individuals in semi-routine or routine occupations who had increased levels of CRP compared with individuals in management and professional occupations.

In conclusion, the measure of SEP you use may lead you to come to different conclusions, and the control variables included may alter the relationship between two variables in unexpected ways.

Further Reading

Harris, K. M., & McDade, T. W. (2018). The biosocial approach to human development, behavior, and health across the life course. *RSF: The Russell Sage Foundation Journal of the Social Sciences, 4*(4), 2–26. https://doi.org/10.7758/RSF.2018.4.4.01

APPENDIX 2

SOFTWARE AND DATA USED IN THIS BOOK AND RELATED USER GUIDES

Software:

SPSS is available from www.ibm.com/uk-en/analytics/spss-statistics-software

SPSS: *IBM SPSS Statistics 25 Core System User's Guide*

STATA is available from www.stata-uk.com

STATA: *Base Reference Manual*

SAS is available from www.sas.com

SAS: *SAS/STAT User Guide*

Data:

Understanding Society: Waves 1–7, 2009–2016 and Harmonised BHPS: Waves 1–18, 1991–2009. [data collection]. 10th Edition. UK Data Service SN: 6614. University of Essex. Institute for Social and Economic Research, NatCen Social Research, Kantar Public. (2018)., http://doi.org/10.5255/UKDA-SN-6614-11

Understanding Society: Waves 2 and 3 Nurse Health Assessment, 2010–2012 [data collection]. 3rd Edition. UK Data Service SN:7251. University of Essex. Institute for Social and Economic Research and National Centre for Social Research, http://doi.org/10.5255/UKDA-SN-7251-3

GLOSSARY

Bias: A problem that results in incorrect estimates being produced from a sample. Results will be too high or too low. This may arise where the sample is not representative of the population.

Case: A case is a unit for which values are captured. When data is collected from a survey, the case is usually a respondent. Most statistics packages show each case in a single row of data.

Categorical variable: A variable that holds values which represent discrete classes of responses. For example, marital status contains the classes (or categories) of single (never married), married, civil partnership, divorced, widowed, and so on.

Clustering: The process of dividing a population into groups and selecting the sample from only some of them. Geographical clustering is common in surveys conducted face to face. The population is split into geographical units, and the sample is selected from only some of them. This is undertaken to reduce the amount of travel the interviewer needs to do.

Codebook: A codebook describes the contents, structure and layout of a data collection. Codebooks begin with basic front matter, including the study title, name of the principal investigator(s), table of contents, and an introduction describing the purpose and format of the codebook. Some codebooks also include methodological details, such as how weights were computed, and data collection instruments, while others, especially with larger or more complex data collections, leave those details for a separate user guide and/or data collection instrument.

Control variables: A control variable is a variable that is included in an analysis in order to account for its effect and therefore distinguish any impact that it has from the effect of another variable which may be of more interest. For example, if we were looking at the impact of having a degree on health amongst adults over 40 years, we might need to consider the impact of age at the same time. Older people tend to be less likely to have a degree and to have poorer health. If we control for age, we can see whether graduate health is generally better than non-graduate health once age has been accounted for.

Cross-sectional data: Cross-sectional data is collected at a single point in time. It has been likened to taking a snapshot.

Dependent variable: A variable (often denoted by y) whose value depends on that of another.

Derived variable: A variable that is created after data collection following some sort of calculation or other processing.

Descriptive statistic: A statistic which simply describes a characteristic of variable for a group of cases. This generally does not have any explanatory power.

Estimate: A statistic, produced using a sample of cases, which is designed to produce information about the characteristics of the population.

External validity: The validity of applying the conclusions of a scientific study outside the context of that study. In other words, it is the extent to which the results of a study can be generalized to and across other situations, people, stimuli and times.

Independent variable: A variable (often denoted by x) whose variation does not depend on that of another.

Likert scale: A type of rating scale used to measure attitudes or opinions.

Longitudinal data: Data that contains information about the same units (usually respondents) over time is called longitudinal data. It can be contrasted with cross-sectional data, which collects data at a single time.

Metadata: A set of data that describes and gives information about other data.

Missing value: A value that is differentiated from a 'valid' response, such as 'did not answer' or 'not applicable'. Missing values are excluded from most procedures.

Multivariate: These are methods that use data from more than two variables at a time, often several variables are included as controls. Statistical modelling is a particularly common form of multivariate method.

Ordinal variable: This a categorical variable that contains values which represent categories which have a natural order. For example, the highest level of qualification might respect an ordering such as higher degree, first degree, further education below degree, GCSE (General Certificate of Secondary Education) or equivalent or no qualification. The values assigned to the classes should respect the natural order.

Paradata: Data about the process by which the data were collected.

Population: A defined set of units, for example, all 'residents in England and Wales in 2011'. The population is the group that we seek to describe.

Primary data: Data that is collected by a researcher from first-hand sources, using methods such as surveys, interviews or experiments. It is collected with the research project in mind, directly from primary sources.

Proxy respondent: A person in a survey or study other than the main subject/ respondent who provides responses about the subject/respondent on their behalf.

Proxy variable: A variable that is not in itself directly relevant, but that serves in place of an unobservable or immeasurable variable. In order for a variable to be a good proxy, it must have a close correlation, not necessarily linear, with the variable of interest.

Raw data: A variable that stores responses given to a question in the survey in their original form.

Replicable study: A study that produces the same results if repeated exactly.

Representative sample: That which replicates the characteristics of the population.

Respondent: A person, or other entity, who responds to a survey.

Sample: A subset of a population.

Sampling frame: The source material or device from which a sample is drawn. It is a list of all those within a population who can be sampled and may include individuals, households or institutions.

Secondary data: Research data that has previously been gathered and can be accessed by researchers.

SAS: A commercial statistics package (see Appendix 2).

SPSS: A commercial statistics package (see Appendix 2).

STATA: A commercial statistics package (see Appendix 2).

Survey non-response: Sample members may not be contactable or may refuse to participate in the survey. Sample members who do not take part in the survey are known as 'non-respondents'.

Unit of analysis: The unit which is being analysed. This is synonymous to the case.

Value: A representation of a characteristic for one case, for one value. In many packages, the value is represented by a number.

Value label: A label associated with a value to enable humans to understand what it means.

Variable: Anything which can vary. In surveys, this is usually a characteristic that varies between cases.

Weighting: A means by which the relative importance of cases can be changed. By default all cases count as one unit. Weighting changes this so that a case with high weight counts more and a case with low weight counts less. The process is usually undertaken in order to fix problems of unrepresentativeness in a sample.

Check out the next title in the collection *Experimental Designs*, for guidance on Types of Experimental Designs.

REFERENCES

Blume, J. & Peipert, J.F. (2003). What your statistician never told you about P-Values, *The Journal of the American Association of Gynecologic Laparoscopists, 10*(4), 439–444. https://doi.org/10.1016/S1074-3804(05)60143-0.

Hakim, C. (1982). Secondary analysis in social research: A guide to data sources and methods with examples. Allen & Unwin/Unwin Hyman.

Scotland, J. (2012). Exploring the philosophical underpinnings of research: Relating ontology and epistemology to the methodology and methods of the scientific, interpretive, and critical research paradigms. *English Language Teaching, 5*(9), 9–16. https://doi.org/10.5539/elt.v5n9p9

Smith, E. (2008). *Using secondary data in educational and social research* (1st ed.) Open University Press.

Wasserstein, R. L., Schirm, A. L., & Lazar, N. A. (2019). Moving to a world beyond '$p < 0.05$'. *The American Statistician, 73*(Suppl. 1), 1–19. https://doi.org/10.1080/00031305.2019.1583913

INDEX

Page numbers in *italic* indicate figures and in **bold** indicate tables.

access to data, 28, 34, 37–8
administrative data sets, 135
Adult Psychiatric Morbidity Survey, 30, 31
'all that apply' questions, 53
alpha test, 82
analysis of variance (ANOVA), 84–7, **84**, **86**
   multivariate, 51, 94–5
   repeated measures, 94–5
   weighted, 90, **91**
attrition, 37, 93, 102

Bartlett's test, **84**, 85, **86**, 87
Bayesian inference, 87
between groups, **84**, 85
bias, 6
big data analysis, 6–7
biomarker data case study, 138–55
   bivariate distributions, 145–50,
      146, **147**, **148**, **149**
   comparing means, 148–9, **149**
   control variables, 140
   cross tabulations, 145–8, **146**, **147**, **148**
   data management, 140–3
   dependent variables, 139–40, 141–2
   descriptive analysis, 150–1, **150–1**
   independent variables, 138–9, 142–3
   multivariate analysis, 150–4, **150–1**, **152**,
      153, **154**
   regression analysis, 151–4, **152**, **153**, **154**
   univariate distributions, 143–5, *143*, **144**,
      144, **145**
bivariate associations, 77–87
   biomarker data case study, 145–50,
      146, **147**, **148**, **149**
   comparing means, 83–7, **84**, *85*, **86**,
      148–9, **149**
   correlations, 81–3, **82**
   cross tabulations, 79–80, **80**, 145–8,
      146, **147**, **148**
   data manipulation, 77–8

Bonferroni correction, 126
Bonferroni test, 87
boost samples, 37, 58, 89
British Birth Cohort Study, 36, 93
British Household Panel Survey (BHPS), 37,
   38, 58, 59, **60**, **61**, *85*
Browne–Forsythe test, 86

cases, 40–1
categorical variables, 71, 74, 77, 81, 83, 100
   biomarker data case study, 139, 144–8, **144**,
      146, **147**, **148**, 150–1, **150–1**, 152,
      153–4, **153**, **154**
census data, 23–4
CESSDA (Consortium of European Social
   Science Data Archives), 2
chi-square test, 124, 145, **146**, 147, 150
citations, 26, 40
CLOSER Learning Hub, 36, 57
clustering, 91, 125
codebooks *see* data documentation
command interfaces, 48
confidence intervals (CIs), 88, 111
consistency, 24–5
CONSORT (Consolidated Standards of
   Reporting Trials) guidelines, 108
content validity, 25
continuous variables, 73, 74, 77, 83,
   100, 113, 115
   biomarker data case study, 139–40, 145,
      145, 148–52, **149**, **150–1**, **152**,
      153, **154**
control variables, 95, 102, 109,
   111, 123, 140
controlled data, 37–8
correlations, 81–3, **82**
Cox models, 87
Crime Survey for England and Wales, 90
criterion validity, 25
critical awareness, 127–8

cross tabulations, 79–80, **80**,
    145–8, **146**, **147**, **148**
cross-sectional studies, 36

data, big, 6–7
data access, 28, 34, 37–8
data archives, 2, 4, 6–7, 22, 36
data collection *see* primary data collection
data documentation, 7–8, 34–5, 36, 38–41, 90
data dredging, 126–7
data formats, 38, 48
data management, 48, 50–7
    common problems, 52–3
    creating subsets of data, 50, 56
    creating variables, 56–7, 78, 98–100
    exercises/examples, 63–6, 77–8,
        95–100, 140–3
    log files, 57
    long-formatted data, 50–2, **51**, 95
    merging data sets, 56, 96–8, 140–1
    ordering data sets, 54
    recoding variables, 57, 65, 77–8, 98, 141
    recording changes, 57
    selecting variables, 55–6, 141
    skip patterns, 52
    sorting data, 56, 65
    summarising data, 65–6
    wide-formatted data, 50–2, **51**, 95
data mining, 127
data search strategies, 25–31
    access to data, 28, 34, 37–8
    internet search engines, 22, 25
    keywords and search terms, 25, 28–9, 30
    literature review, 26, 30
    narrowing down search results, 27–8, 30–1
    UKDS search tools, 26–8, 30
data storage, 134
data structure, 38–40
    derived variables, 39–40, 122–3
    identifiers, 38–9, 40, 60, **62**
    key variables, 40, 55–6, 61, **62–3**, 63
    variable naming conventions, 39–40
data subset creation, 50, 56
dependent variables, 16, 23, 24
derived variables, 39–40, 122–3
descriptive analysis, 100–2, **101**,
    150–1, **150–1**
digital object identifiers (DOIs), 26
documentation *see* data documentation

Economic and Social Research Council (ESRC),
    2, 134
English Longitudinal Study of Ageing (ELSA),
    17, 37, 48, 54–7, 93
epistemological issues, 4–5
ethical concerns, 133–4
ethnic minority groups, 5–6, 37, 58, 89, 121–2

EU General Data Protection Regulation, 133
European Quality of Life Survey, 42–5, *43*, *44*
European Social Survey, 2
Excel, 114
explanatory variables *see* independent
    variables
external validity, 5

face validity, 25, 35
factor analysis, 82
federated access management, 38
fixed effects, 51
full information maximum likelihood (FIML),
    125, 126
funding agencies, 2, 134–5

general linear model (GLM), 94–5
GESIS – Leibniz-Institute for the Social
    Sciences, 2
Government Office Regions (GORs), 52
graphs, preparing, 111, *113*, 115–16, *115*, *116*
grossing weights, 89–91, **91**
growth curve models, 51

Health Survey for England (HSE), 30, 36, 122
Humanities and Social Science Electronic
    Thesaurus (HASSET), 29, 30

identifiers, 38–9, 40, 60, **62**
independent variables, 16, 24
inferential statistics, 5, 87–8
informed consent, 133
internet search engines, 22, 25
Inter-University Consortium for Political and
    Social Research (ICPSR), 2

key variables, 40, 55–6, 61, **62–3**, 63
keywords and search terms, 25, 28–9, 30
Kruskal–Wallis test, 86

Labour Force Survey (LFS), 36, 38, 90
Levene's test, 86
licence agreements, 28, 37–8
Likert scales, 70
limitations of secondary data analysis, 120–9
linear regression analysis, 102–4, **103**, 128,
    151–2, **152**, 153, **154**
literature review, 13, 14, 16, 26, 30
log files, 57
logistic regression analysis, 124, 152, 153–4,
    153, **154**
long-formatted data, 50–2, **51**, 95
longitudinal data analysis, 93–104
    associations between variables, 93–4
    data management, 95–100
    descriptive analysis, 100–2, **101**,
        150–1, **150–1**

modelling changes in repeated
measures, 94–5
regression analysis, 102–4, **103**, 151–4,
152, **153**, **154**
see also biomarker data case study
longitudinal studies, 36–7, 52–3, 93

marginal multilevel models, 94–5
means, comparing, 83–7, **84**, *85*, **86**,
148–9, **149**
merging data sets, 56, 96–8, 140–1
metadata, 7
Millennium Cohort Study (MCS),
36, 93, 135
missing data, 123–6
missing at random (MAR), 125
missing completely at random (MCAR),
124–5
missing not at random, 125–6
missing values/missing value codes, 36, 39,
52, 53, 55, 61, **61**, 77
mixed models, 51, 94–5
multiple imputation, 125, 126
multivariate analysis of variance (MANOVA),
51, 94–5
multivariate associations, 87–93
biomarker data case study, 150–4, **150–1**,
152, **153**, **154**
statistical inference, 87–8
stratification, 91–3, **92**
weighting, 88–93, **91**, **92**

National Child Development Study (NCDS),
36, 38, 93
National Statistics Socio-Economic
Classification (NS-SEC), 138–9
Nesstar Catalogue, 31, 36, 42–5, *43*, *44*
non-coverage, 89
non-response, 88, 89, 123, 124–5
'nowcasting' methods, 22

objectivism, 4–5
observational research, 108
ONS Longitudinal Study (ONS LS), 37, 93
ontological issues, 4–5
open data licences, 37, 134
ordinal variables *see* categorical variables
outcome variables *see* dependent variables

p values, 88, 110, 111, 126, 127–8
panel studies, 37, 93
paradata, 7–8, 121
path analyses, 51
Pearson correlation, 81
p-hacking, 88
population, 5, 17, 23, 35
positivism, 4–5

post-stratification, 89
practical exercises and examples
comparing means, 83–7, **84**, *85*, **86**
correlations, 81–3, **82**
cross tabulations, 79–80, **80**
data management, 63–6, 77–8,
95–100, 140–3
descriptive analysis, 100–2, **101**
regression analysis, 102–4, **103**
stratification, **92**, 93
univariate distributions, 71–7,
72, *74*, **75**, **76**
weighting, 90, **91**, **92**, 93
writing up results, 112–16, **112**,
113, **114–15**, *115*, *116*
see also biomarker data case study
primary data collection, 2, 35
bias, 6
boost samples, 37, 58, 89
context of, 7, 36–7
cross-sectional studies, 36
documentation, 7–8, 35, 36, 38–41, 90
ethical concerns, 133
interviews, 6, 7, 35, 41
longitudinal studies, 36–7, 52–3, 93
metadata, 7
paradata, 7–8, 121
population representation, 17, 23, 35
questionnaires, 35, 41
sample size, 24, 35, 40–1, 110, 121–2
skip patterns, 52
subjectivity, 6
time and resources, 4
units of, 37, 40
primary data sources, 3
primary sampling units (PSUs), 91
principal component analysis (PCA), 82
PRISMA (Preferred Reporting Items for
Systematic Reviews and Meta-Analyses)
guidelines, 108
probability weights, 89
proxy respondents, 39
proxy variables, 121

question banks, 24, 25, 31

raw data, 70
realism, 4–5
registration, 38
regression analysis
linear, 102–4, **103**, 128, 151–2,
152, 153, **154**
logistic, 124, 152, 153–4, **153**, **154**
reliability, 24–5, 35
repeated measures, modelling changes in,
94–5
replicable studies, 5

report writing *see* writing up results
representative samples, 17, 23, 35
research design, 12–17
  concepts and measurements, 14–16
  ideal data set, 22–5
  population representation, 17, 23, 35
  research questions, 12–13, 22, 35, 126–7
  research topic, 13, 22
  units of analysis, 17, 23, 51
  see also data search strategies
research results *see* writing up results
response rates, 35
Roper Center for Public
  Opinion Research, 2

safeguarded data, 37, 38
sample attrition, 37, 93, 102
sampling design/strategies
  boost samples, 37, 58, 89
  documentation, 40–1
  population representation, 17, 23, 35
  primary sampling units (PSUs), 91
  sample size, 24, 35, 40–1, 110, 121–2
  simple random sampling, 88–9
  stratification, 91–3, **92**, 125
  units of data collection, 37, 40
  weighting, 88–93, **91**, **92**, 122, 125, 126
sampling frames, 89
SAS, 48, 57, 77
scatter plots, 115–16, *115*, *116*
Scheffé test, **86**, 87
scientific paradigm, 4–5
search engines
  internet, 22, 25
  UKDS, 27–8, 30
searching for data *see* data search strategies
secondary data analysis
  advantages, 3–4
  definition, 3
  ethical concerns, 133–4
  limitations, 120–9
Šidák test, 87
significance testing, 88, 127–8
skip patterns, 52
Smith, Emma, 35–6
social construction of data, 5–6
SPSS, 48
  .sps files, 57
  command interface, 48
SPSS commands, 49
  COMPUTE, 49
  CROSSTABS, 49
  DESCRIPTIVES, 49, 76
  FREQUENCIES, 49, 74
  IF, 49
  KEEP, 54
  LIST, 49

RECODE, 49
SELECT IF, 49
SORT CASES, 49
Standard Statistical Regions, 52
STATA, 48
  .do files, 57
  .log files, 57
  command interface, 48
  installing commands, 74–5
STATA commands, 49–50, 63–6
  alpha, 82
  browse, 65
  codebook, 64
  compress, 96, 97
  count if, 64
  describe, 64
  drop, 96, 97, 100, 140
  drop if, 50, 98
  duplicates, 64
  egen, 83
  fre, 74–6, 83
  gen, 57, 78, 79, 83, 98–9, 142
  generate, 50
  gsort, 65
  histogram/hist, 87, 113, 143
  inspect, 64
  isid, 64
  keep, 73, 96, 97, 141
  keep if, 50, 96, 97, 98, 141
  label, 99–100, 142–3
  list, 64–5
  log, 57
  logit, 152, 153
  merge, 96, 97, 140–1
  mvdecode, 65
  oneway, 84, 87, 90, 148–9
  order, 54
  pwcorr, 81
  recode, 65, 77, 78, 79, 98,
    99, 141, 142, 148
  regress, 151, 153
  replace ... if, 50, 57, 65, 83, 99
  save, 96, 97
  save as, 55
  sort, 50, 56, 96, 97
  sum, 76, 100
  summ, 76, 142, 145
  summarize, 50, 65
  svy, 93, 102–3, 151, 152, 153
  svyset, 93, 102, 151
  tab, 96, 97
  tab1, 100, 144
  tab2, 79–80, 145, 147, 150
  table, 66
  tabstat, 66, 114
  tabulate, 50, 65–6
  ttest, 150

twoway, 115–16
use, 54, 63–4, 73, 96, 97, 140
xi, 151, 152, 153
statistical inference, 5, 87–8
statistical significance, 88, 127–8
stratification and strata, 91–3, **92**, 125
STROBE (Strengthening the Reporting of
    Observational studies in Epidemiology)
    guidelines, 108
subjectivity, 5–6
survey documentation *see* data
    documentation
survey non-response, 88, 89, 123
Survey of Health and Retirement
    in Europe, 2
survey question banks, 24, 25, 31
survival analysis, 51
syntax repositories, 128–9

t test, 111, 150
tables, preparing, 111, 113–15, **114–15**
theories and hypotheses, 6

UK Data Service (UKDS), 2, 7
    access to data, 28, 37–8
    key data pages, 27
    Nesstar Catalogue, 31, 36, 42–5, *43*, *44*
    registration, 38
    search tools, 26–8, 30
    syntax repository, 128–9
    theme pages, 27
    variable and question bank, 31
Understanding Society (UKHLS)
    data set, 48, 57–66, 93, 135
    access to data, 59
    boost sample, 37, 58
    data files, 38, 59, **60**
    identifiers, 60, **62**
    key variables, 61, **62–3**, 63
    missing value codes, 61, **61**
    population and samples, 58
    unit of data collection, 37
    variable names, 60–1
    weighting variables, 90
    see also biomarker data case study;
        practical exercises and examples

units of analysis, 17, 23, 51
units of data collection, 37, 40
univariate distributions, 70–7, *72*, *74*, **75**, **76**
    biomarker data case study, 143–5,
        143, **144**, *144*, **145**
user guides *see* data documentation

validity, 24–5, 35
    content, 25
    criterion, 25
    external, 5
    face, 25, 35
value labels, 52
variables, 8, 14–16
    common problems, 52–3
    creating, 56–7, 78, 98–100
    dependent, 16, 23, 24
    derived, 39–40, 122–3
    identifiers, 38–9, 40, 60, **62**
    independent, 16, 24
    key, 40, 55–6, 61, **62–3**, 63
    missing values/missing value codes, 36, 39,
        52, 53, 55, 61, **61**, 77
    naming conventions, 39–40
    non-intuitive names, 52
    proxy, 121
    raw data, 70
    recoding, 57, 65, 77–8, 98, 141
    selecting, 55–6, 141
    value labels, 52
    weighting, 88–93, **91**, **92**, 122, 125, 126
    see also categorical variables; continuous
        variables

weighting, 88–93, **91**, **92**, 122, 125, 126
Whitehall II Study, 93
wide-formatted data, 50–2, **51**, 95
within groups, **84**, 85
writing up results, 108–16
    guidelines, 108–10
    practical exercise, 112–16, **112**, *113*,
        114–15, *115*, *116*
    preparing graphs, 111, *113*, 115–16, *115*,
        116
    preparing tables, 111, 113–15, **114–15**
    using text, 110

CPSIA information can be obtained
at www.ICGtesting.com
Printed in the USA
JSHW042207230522
26107JS00004B/92